HAPPINESS UNLIMITED

HAPPINESS UNLIMITED

AWAKENING *with* BRAHMA KUMARIS

Sister
BK SHIVANI
in conversation with
Suresh Oberoi

AMARYLLIS

AMARYLLIS

An imprint of Manjul Publishing House Pvt. Ltd.
• 7/32, Ansari Road, Daryaganj, New Delhi 110 002
Website: www.manjulindia.com
Registered Office:
• 10, Nishat Colony, Bhopal 462 003 – India

Happiness Unlimited
Awakening with Brahma Kumaris

This edition first published in 2019
Second impression 2020

ISBN 978-93-88241-89-2

Cover design by Neha Behl

Printed and bound in India by Thomson Press (India) Ltd.

CONTENTS

HAPPINESS UNLIMITED

The reason there is so little happiness in the world is dependency. And this is the irony—because happiness is not dependent on 'anything' or 'anyone' or found 'anywhere'.

Happiness is only possible when we are able to accept everyone as they are. That means an end to judging or resisting others, an end to complaining and blaming, an end to criticising and controlling, and an end to competing with anyone.

It is only when we choose thoughts and feelings aligned with our true state of purity, peace and love that we shift from asking to sharing; holding on to letting go; expectations to acceptance; the past and the future to being in the now. We create a life of joy, contentment and bliss, because we have the choice and the power. Happiness is a decision.

That is the thought motif that will be pursued in the conversation that is to unfold between Suresh Oberoi, the internationally recognised Indian cinema actor, and Sister

Shivani, a practitioner of Rajyoga Meditation of the Brahma Kumaris. By no means is it a linear conversation. Moments of clarity intersperse with mirages of certain bliss—but that distinction is precisely what the mind has to move toward grasping.

This is not a word-for-word transliteration of the interview. Through this book, we are trying to capture the essence of Sister Shivani's thoughts and understanding of *Happiness* and its various dimensions.

INTRODUCTION

The international spiritual and motivational flagship show *Awakening with Brahma Kumaris* has continued to change millions of minds for over a decade, and has been spreading its wings far and wide to the ends of the planet. Even if only for 30 minutes a day, the daily talk show has answers to life's probing and insightful questions. At the helm of the show is the globally acclaimed authority figure in spiritual and emotional empowerment, Sister BK Shivani, whose profound and practical wisdom has made millions of viewers think, understand, introspect, experiment, take positive steps forward, and experience self-transformation. The peace, love and compassion that she embodies reflect in her timeless messages shared through the platform.

With over 2,000 episodes between 2007 and today, the *Awakening* programme has explored more than 20 wide-ranging series themed around upliftment of human consciousness.

Not just a household name within India, the show has left prominent footprints in USA, UK, Europe, Asia, Middle East, Africa, Australia and New Zealand. Viewers have been successfully overcoming self-defeating behaviours leading to mental stress, depression, addictions, low self-esteem and troubled relationships. They have realized their inner power, become resilient, feel good about themselves, and have taken responsibility for their everyday life.

The essence of knowledge shared on the platform is an offshoot of the teachings of the Brahma Kumaris, a spiritual organization headquartered at Mount Abu, India, and the largest to be led by women. The seed of service was planted in 1937, and today has sprouted into as many 4,500 centres in over 140 countries across 5 continents. The institution is accredited with General Consultative Status with the United Nations Economic and Social Council (ECOSOC). It also holds Associate Status with the Department of Public Information (DPI), Consultative Status with United Nations Children's Fund (UNICEF), and Observer Status to the United Nations Environment Assembly of UNEP. It supports UN programmes on a wide range of developmental, humanitarian and other issues.

The teachings of Brahma Kumaris are derived from the ancient spiritual wisdom of Rajyoga but perfectly relevant in today's times. Everyone explores their own spirituality and learn skills of reflection and meditation derived from Rajyoga, which will help develop inner calm, clear thinking and personal well-being. With a commitment to make spiritual education accessible to everyone, Brahma Kumaris welcomes people from all walks of life, irrespective of age, faith and background.

Anyone can simply walk in to their nearest centre and fix a time convenient to them to learn Rajyoga meditation. The foundation course is a 7-day programme of 1 hour per day, offered *free of charge*. People are also welcome to attend the spiritual study class conducted worldwide every day. Several other courses are offered to individuals and corporates through dialogues, community projects, interfaith programmes, lectures, workshops, seminars, conferences and other platforms.

Website: http://www.brahmakumaris.org
Centres in India: https://www.brahmakumaris.com/centers/
Centers Worldwide: http://www.brahmakumaris.org/centre-locator

A NOTE TO THE READER

Dear Happy Soul,

Om Shanti. Greetings of peace and happiness.

The fact that you are reading this book is a testimony of your desire and determination to ingrain happiness into your personality. Congratulations on taking the first step. It is humbly intended that these pages help you find, understand, experience and express the kind of happiness you desire.

When I first embarked on the journey of *Awakening With Brahma Kumaris*, it was easy to trace back all the unhappiness in our world to the sadness in our own minds. From children to young adults to senior citizens, everyone was inundated with chaos in both inner and outer worlds. Everyone was looking for happiness, but many were unsure where, how and when to find it. The need to provide a new vantage point, a bright way of looking at life, is what sparked the idea to discuss happiness at length, as a central theme.

That is how the television series *Happiness Unlimited* came about. With around 30 episodes under its hat, the conversations cut through every facet, every layer of what happiness entails. The show garnered an overwhelming response from the audience across the world. In a way, it was looked upon as the answer, a go-to guide, a solution, for the quest and craving for peace and happiness by individuals, families and societies.

An emotion as rich as happiness takes time for anyone to meaningfully and completely reflect, churn, ingrain, adopt into their lifestyle and gain mastery. For this reason, viewers of the TV show needed a constant guide by the side as they sustained, pondered, discovered, and implemented the take-aways from what they watched on television.

May this book be a gift that keeps on giving. Whether you are in the comfort of your home, at office, commuting, or on a vacation, these pages offer ways to find day-to-day experience of happiness, no matter what circumstance you are in. As you add this book to your spiritual library, as you read, rethink and reprogramme your mind to tune in to a happy frequency, pause and notice how life all around you improves in drastic ways.

BK Shivani

CHAPTER ONE

FINDING HAPPINESS: A REALITY CHECK

There is a time to bid good-bye to the old and the ordinary, and to awaken the beauty within. That time is now. It is time to wake up and take charge of life and rethink refreshingly. Indeed, it is time to Awaken with Brahma Kumaris.
Om Shanti!

Suresh Oberoi: Why is so much emphasis laid on Happiness as a topic?
Sister Shivani: Attaining happiness has been the most common human pursuit as we build our lives. In who we are, what we do, where we go, how we perform—the bottom line has been to seek and experience happiness. Discussing it as a topic helps us to understand the emotion in its entirety, so as to create real and lasting happiness.

SO: We are looking for happiness, as you said. But what is it through which we are looking for it?

SS: The channels through which most of us look for happiness is interesting. It ranges from position, possessions, property, relationships, health and so on. Today if you ask someone what they want in life, they say success. But they want success essentially because they believe it makes them happy. Likewise, ask them why they own or purchase material comfort, and the most likely response is that it makes them or their family happy. And the biggest reason people get into relationships today is to get that sense of happiness from the other person. So, finally everyone is looking for just that one feeling—happiness.

SO: Happiness derived out of these means is limited, isn't it?

SS: It is. In fact, we really need to check if any of them can even give us happiness.

SO: It is momentary—like a child who breaks one toy and then wants another toy, and then yet another. What are we looking for? If we are looking for happiness, shouldn't it be permanent?

SS: By itself, happiness should be a permanent and lasting emotion. When it comes naturally to us, we won't be dependent on anything outside. But the moment we make happiness dependent on something, it becomes a fleeting emotion.

Simply put, if you look for happiness outside of you, you are dependent on a situation to be favourable. Happiness now becomes conditional and fleeting. If I am happy only when the weather is pleasant, my feeling good is dependent on the weather. I will not allow myself to feel nice if it gets hotter or colder.

SO: How can one be happy without desires and dependencies?
SS: That's probably one of the oldest belief systems we have allowed ourselves to live by—the belief that happiness is to be acquired from the outside, whether it's from achievements or from people or from what we are. The equation has been 'I am doing this so that I will feel happy'. Only when it's done, and done perfectly, I can be happy. So, the dependency is on the act being performed in the right manner. This belief is ingrained right from childhood. Parents feel good when the child gets good marks, when the child performs well, when the child dresses up well, and so on.

Slowly a child is conditioned to believe that he is responsible for his parents' happiness. If they are happy, he can be happy too, and not otherwise.

SO: Can you share the meaning of happiness and explain how to experience it without any dependency?
SS: First and foremost, let's see the factors we have made it dependent on. The simplest dependency that we experience on a daily basis is on objects. We say 'I'll feel happy when I buy a new car; I'll feel happy when I buy new property; I am happy when I go shopping.'

SO: But what is wrong in this? Isn't this natural?
SS: What is more important is—Is there truth in this? Are these dependencies actually making us happy?

SO: I certainly will be happy if I buy a new car.

SS: Of course, you will, but is it the car that is giving you the happiness you are looking for?

I will be happy when I have a new car... which means, if I don't, then there's a question mark on my happiness. This also means that 10 days down the line, if the car gets a scratch or a bump, my happiness is again going to get affected, because I have conditioned myself into believing that it is the car that is giving me happiness. Now that is not true. You buy a new car—the most expensive car in the world. I feel comfortable sitting in the car. So who is experiencing the comfort? It's the body. Plush seats, the best music system and a powerful AC. There is flawless physical comfort. I feel comfortable sitting in the car and tell myself that I am feeling good. Suppose at that moment I get a phone call giving me news of an unpleasant situation at home. Will I still be happy?

SO: No, I cannot be.

SS: But I am still comfortable. I am still in the most comfortable car. Here we need to understand that the car was designed to give me physical comfort and it will continue to give me physical comfort, irrespective of my situations.

SO: Are happiness and comfort two different things?

SS: Yes. Anything physical is designed to give me physical comfort. The chair I am sitting on is physical and giving me physical comfort, but I wrongly believed it gave me happiness.

SO: Is this a wrong belief that we have?
SS: We have been conditioned to believe so, right from childhood. We have grown up with it. But now we need to question our belief system.

SO: Parents buy things for children or take them out often, believing it makes the child happy.
SS: Absolutely. Today we live in luxurious homes and drive the swankiest cars. We have all the possessions we desired. We have every gadget we wanted. Then why are we still looking for happiness? Shouldn't the search have ended with all objects of comfort? You name it and we have it all. But we still seem to be searching for that feeling, which the objects of comfort are unable to give. What we have got from them is a comfortable life.

SO: In the context of the car, the comfort is also not felt when there is a phone call about something unpleasant at home.
SS: Visualize yourself in the car, seated comfortably and enjoying the drive. It is your mind that suddenly creates pain because of the phone call. It is always mind over matter. When the mind is in pain, physical comfort becomes immaterial. My body is comfortable—but 'I' am uncomfortable at that moment.

I am looking for happiness. So, at that moment the physical comfort does not matter. It could be the other way around too. I may be uncomfortable physically, I may just be sitting cross-legged on the floor, but internally I can feel bliss, and so I feel very comfortable.

SO: How does one get there?

SS: By understanding that physical comfort is separate from emotional comfort. Suppose I was not able to experience internal comfort—the internal stability that we call happiness, and I believe if I am physically comfortable, I will be happy. Today, we have started trying to buy happiness. If I buy this and that... the list is never ending—I will be happy. It doesn't mean we don't buy things; it just means we don't associate objects with our being happy. Let's buy things for their utility or comfort, not for happiness.

I need clarity about why I buy something, so that I don't tell my mind it gives me happiness. If I associate material objects with happiness, then I would only keep postponing happiness by putting new conditions. Suppose I am constructing a house. I tell myself that once the house is built and I shift there, I will be happy. This could take a year or two so I postpone my happiness until a distant future. Think of a child—we look at the child in school and say childhood is the best phase of life, but the child looks at grownups and says they are lucky, for they don't have projects or exams. The child is looking to be out of school so that he can be happy. He feels he will be very happy when he goes to a college. Then, when he gets into a college, he feels he will be happy once he starts earning... and then marriage and then family.... Even after all that, he feels he can be happy once his children settle well. Few years down the line, the children also settle well and everything is fine. What is his thought now? He feels he will be very happy when he retires. So, when will he actually be happy?

He kept postponing happiness to different stages of life, and every time there was a new blank to fill in. This is how we get into a vicious circle: *when this happens, I will be happy.*

SO: How distressing!
SS: True! And that's why we are not happy.

SO: We find extremely wealthy individuals owning private aircrafts and million-dollar yachts seeking happiness. How does one put an end to this search?
SS: First, by understanding that happiness is separate from physical comforts. Second, by understanding that happiness is my internal creation and I can create it irrespective of everything else. I buy a car and then I say I am happy. The car is a physical object with no feelings or emotions. Obviously, the car is not giving me happiness. But what else is? I create the thought: 'Wow! I bought a car. I finally bought what I wanted.' These are positive thoughts.

Another example is when someone buys a piece of jewellery. Does jewellery give her happiness? Or it is her positive thought she creates about possessing that piece?

SO: The positive thought cannot be created without the jewellery.
SS: It means I need an object as a stimulus to create a response. So, it's the object, and the object can be anything, like the jewellery set or a car. I look at the object and I create a thought within. So when we acquire an object, our natural response

is 'This is a lovely piece of jewellery that I have just got'. Now who created this thought?

SO: That's tricky. Did I create the thought or was it created because of the object?
SS: A physical piece of jewellery does not have thoughts and feelings. I look at it and I create a thought—'I have bought such a lovely piece of jewellery!'

If somebody walks into the room 10 minutes later and says it is not nice or says it is fake, what happens then? Now who is creating the response? If the stimulus was creating the response, then the stimulus will keep on creating the same response, irrespective of a change in situation. Further, if I show the same piece of jewellery to 10 people, will all of them create the same thoughts? Someone says—It's too loud. Another may say—I am sorry, I don't like jewellery. A third friend might say—I love it but I can't afford it. The piece of jewellery is the same.

SO: My response to the piece is my choice.
SS: Yes, it is in my thought.

SO: I am responding, which means I am creating. I am creating either happiness or unhappiness.
SS: We could create thoughts of pleasure or thoughts of jealousy or hurt in response to the same piece of jewellery. The stimulus is the same, the object is the same. If the object were to create the thought, it would create the same thought in everyone.

If the object—whether a car, a piece of jewellery, or a lovely garden—is what is creating the thought, then it should create the same thought in every person. Look at the greenery around this place. You may admire nature, while another person may just walk past it without acknowledging its beauty.

These are different responses to the same stimulus. The response is the choice of the creator and I am the creator.

SO: I am the creator and I am creating unhappiness or happiness. But how does one do without a stimulus?
SS: By understanding that I am creating the thought. We were not aware that we are the creators. We believed thoughts come to us because of something outside.

If you say something that I believe is rude I get hurt. I may not even realize that I am creating that feeling of hurt. I conveniently say—You hurt me. I think it is all coming from outside. So I expect that you need to speak politely for me to feel better. I wait for you to apologize because once you do that, I would feel better. This is dependency.

SO: Perhaps I would say I never meant that.
SS: But I will still say you hurt me. We can go on telling people—I am hurt because of you… I am angry because of you… I am upset because of you… I am jealous because of you… I am happy because of you.

SO: If everything is happening because of others, I am not taking personal responsibility.
SS: No responsibility and no control. We live like victims if we are constantly dependent on external circumstances.

SO: Isn't that a weakness?
SS: But isn't that the way we are living? The minute we understand they are not controlling us and we are not dependent on them, we will have a choice. This is independence. The first thing spirituality gives us is freedom. It liberates us from all dependencies, from everything we thought we were dependent on and postponed our happiness. We convinced ourselves that we could not be happy until we had what we wanted.

SO: How I can be happy without having what I want?
SS: We talked about objects, but what about achievements? We say—'I wanted to achieve this goal but I haven't reached there, so how can I be happy?' We have been brought up to believe that only those achievers can be happy.

SO: Isn't it natural? If I fail to get a job three times in a row, isn't it normal to be unhappy?
SS: I thought that my happiness was dependent on getting a job. I thought it was normal and that's why getting upset was a normal reaction too. To be tense is normal, to worry is normal, to fear is normal, to be sad is normal, but to feel happy doesn't come so easily to us. Problems and challenges are bound to arise, but to despair or to face them optimistically is our choice. Situations are outside.

SO: But that external scenario disturbs me internally.
SS: That's a choice. Does it disturb everyone? Faced with failure, someone could be upset, someone could commit suicide, and

yet another one would say 'Never mind, let me try again,' and be successful the next time. Same situation, different responses.

That is why my thoughts and feelings are in my control. This understanding will change the way I live.

SO: Between the moment when something happens and you react, there is hardly any time to choose your response.
SS: That's why we are living in an automated mode, just as how a machine functions. What's the difference between a machine and a human being?

A machine has no choice. It is dependent on the person operating it. When you press a button, it has to turn on. You press the button again and it has to turn off. That machine has no other choice. But we human beings have a choice. Someone says something to me—they press an emotional button. If I am a machine, I can say 'obviously I will get angry.' But I am a human being, so there is no compulsion of an obvious response. I have a choice.

Obvious holds good for a machine because it is designed to work in automated ways.

SO: But everybody is living in an automated mode except maybe saints and a few others.
SS: It's not about saints. It's all about being aware that we are human beings and we have a choice. People are pressing our emotional buttons but we have a choice.

SO: Do share about the daily meditation you practice. Does that help you to understand the difference between what is

happening outside and what you are creating within? The perception is that meditation is about zero thoughts. It's difficult not to think.

SS: Meditation is not about stopping the thinking process. It is about becoming aware of my thoughts and choosing my thoughts.

SO: How to be aware of what I am thinking?
SS: Yes, just as we are aware of what we are speaking.

SO: I am not aware.
SS: You are not speaking in an automated mode. You choose what to speak, you choose your actions—when to sit, when to get up, when to walk, when to sleep.

We are choosing our actions, our words. Of course, sometimes the thoughts come racing, so we feel even the words are automated. Sometimes we apologize to people as—'I didn't mean to say that.' The next step will be to become aware of my thoughts, to choose my thoughts and thereby choose my responses. It's a simple exercise we begin every morning and can do it any time during the day—to just watch our thoughts. Sit back and reflect on these thoughts:

> *What am I thinking right now: it could be about work, about family, about friends, about myself. Let me look at my thoughts… look at myself during the whole day: driving to work, reaching my desk, interacting with people… I am doing everything but I am choosing what to do and I am choosing how to be while I am doing it…*

I have a choice how to feel while I am doing everything I am doing outside.... Situations, targets, goals, people— they are all external.... Let me look at myself: how I think, how I feel, and then how I respond.... It's my choice... I am the creator of my response. Om Shanti!

MANTRAS FOR HAPPINESS UNLIMITED

- Happiness is not dependent on physical objects.
- Objects, possessions, gadgets, etc., are designed to give us physical comfort.
- Physical comfort is different from emotional comfort.
- Happiness is emotional comfort. It is our internal creation and can be created irrespective of physical comforts.
- We use objects as a stimulus to create a response, but the response is our choice. Different people create different responses for the same stimulus.
- Problems come, challenges will show up, but to despair or face them optimistically is our choice.

CHAPTER TWO

THE WAYS WE MISS OUT ON HAPPINESS

SO: It is 'I' who create my happiness or sadness. I am responsible. How can I be happy if I have not achieved something in life?

SS: There are two dynamics here: One, if I achieve this, then I will be happy. Second, I will be happy while achieving this.

Suppose we are on a journey from X to Y. When we begin the journey, people wish us and say 'Have a safe journey'. They don't say 'Reach your destination in any way'. It's not only reaching the destination, it's the quality of the journey that counts.

SO: Many of us believe we just have to reach our destination, 'by hook or by crook'.

SS: Let's look at it this way. I set a goal for myself, whether marks as a student, as a professional or in my relationships. We set specific goals at every stage, and without goals we become passive. I wouldn't know where I am heading.

The other thing I do is tell myself I will be happy when I reach the goal. The goal may take six months or six years. Suppose I aim at reaching a certain designation at my workplace in the coming two years. I start my journey. I focus on my projects, my performance and my rapport with colleagues. But at the back of my mind is this thought, that only when I reach there, I will be happy. Somewhere down the line if my performance dips a little, or if my colleagues aren't co-operative, or if any other obstacle comes my way, what happens to me?

SO: I will not be happy.
SS: I create stress, I create anxiety. Why? Because people are coming in the way of my happiness. I see them as obstacles not just to my goal, but to my happiness. I walk from here to there and my mind says my happiness is there. While I am walking, you are in the way, and because you are in the way I see you as someone standing in the way of my happiness. I might choose to do anything to get you out of the way—If you are a junior, I might order you to work faster. If you are a peer, I might consider you to be a threat, and I can plot against you to get you out of my way. I might even compromise on my values by telling a lie to take a shortcut. This means I begin to think that living by my values and principles can delay my happiness.

SO: As long as you get happiness, how does it matter if you were to lie?

SS: At this moment we are still on the journey; we haven't reached the destination yet. While on the journey, I am creating anger and stress, and I am compromising on my values and principles. I am creating negative emotions in the course of my journey. For six months I create anxiety and stress, which in turn can disturb my relationships and create issues with people at work. My emotional turmoil will eventually start affecting my physical health. Finally, when I reach my goal after six months, how will I feel?

SO: Don't you think you will be happy?

SS: I have created all these negative emotions on the way and radiated them emotions to everyone around me. It is like I have fallen down, hurt myself, and by the time I reached there, I am emotionally bruised. But because I have reached there, I am very happy. My conditioning says happiness is dependent on achievements.

SO: You may apologize to family for having late nights or being irritable.

SS: If you set a six-month goal, for the entire duration you are allowing yourself to get bruised and hurt emotionally.

SO: We are not just postponing happiness, we are creating unhappiness and multiplying it.

SS: Exactly. In the first six months, to reach (A) I was bruised because I created negative emotions around me, hurt people, lost my temper, whatever. By the time I reach (A), my emotional strength has dipped. Subsequently in going from (A) to (B), I become weaker. It is the same environment, same people, same situations, but a weak me. It means I am going to get bruised further.

SO: Are you referring to emotional strength?
SS: Yes, my power to face situations. I will get hurt more easily, I will react impulsively, and I will get irritated often.

SO: These behaviors make you physically weak too.
SS: It's certainly going to affect the body, but when we are young, we don't feel the impact. We think it is fine, natural, and the way to live. It takes a few years for the body to start showing symptoms of hypertension, diabetes or other illnesses. Since we accepted stress as a part of life, we also accept physical symptoms and illnesses as inevitable.

SO: I am still not clear how someone can be happy without achieving goals. He comes home with problems, as a failure.
SS: Let's say I have been looking for a job for six months. I have not been getting it and so I become demotivated and upset. As a friend, what would you say to me?

SO: Don't worry, such things happen. You will get a job soon.
SS: If I ask how can I not be worried, what will you say?

SO: By worrying, will you get it?

SS: Exactly. We just need to say this to ourselves: By worrying, will I get a job?

SO: Easier said than done.

SS: But that's the solution. The more I worry, the weaker my mind becomes. It starts to show in my body language. I lose motivation. I need confidence. I need to be enthusiastic. I need to be ready to seize opportunities. It's not about what has happened, it's about what I need to do now—how does my state of being have to be? I have to take care of that without getting trapped in a viciously negative cycle. Who would employ a demotivated individual? Who would like to hire an irritable, weak, intolerant and dispirited employee?

Whatever the situation, whatever the challenge, I cannot get a solution unless I take care of myself. If my business is not doing well and I worry, I will still not be able to do any better. If I want to do well outside, I will have to be well within. More importantly: even if I don't do well, at least I can take care of myself.

SO: My guru told me about a man who was worried about a legal case he was fighting. He was also worried about his wife who was very sick. He won the case after 15 years and even his wife recovered. But he himself fell sick and died.

SS: It's about priorities in life. What are my responsibilities? We normally consider family, job, finances, relationships, friends, country....

We can take care of everything else except taking our own

responsibility. Let's say we are a family of five, and four of them are unwell. If I want to be their caretaker, I need to be healthy myself. This is about physical health. The same applies to emotional health—I want to take care of my children, my spouse, my parents. I want to ensure that they are happy. But I cannot do it if I am in pain.

SO: **I even get sad when my children are not able to do well in class. I wanted them to be swimmers, tennis players, and so on.**
SS: Why? For their happiness. Finally, I want everyone around me to be happy.

SO: **And if they are happy, I will be happy.**
SS: Spirituality teaches us that when I am happy and then take care of them, they will also be happy.

SO: **Being happy I radiate my energy. So I can make others happy too.**
SS: Because you make them stronger. Let's see, what is happiness? Happiness is internal strength. It does not mean excitement. I am not going to be jumping and dancing the whole day. I have lost my job and I am not excited about it.

SO: **Happiness is strength?**
SS: At any given point in time, there can only be one thought in our mind. One thought possesses one quality. That one quality could be either the right quality or the not-so-right quality. If I am creating a pure, powerful and positive thought, then it is the right quality. If I am creating a negative thought,

an unpleasant thought, a thought of anxiety, pain and worry, it's a wrong thought. If it's the right thought I feel good; if it's not the right thought I feel low. If it's the right thought, then I feel good and that is stability. If it is not the right thought, I feel low and that is weakness.

SO: So, stability is strength.
SS: If you are stable, you are strong. This strength will then shape the way you respond to situations. You said, 'I want my child to have good marks'. But that may not happen every time. When he fails to score the expected marks, or the score he is capable of getting, what is your state of mind? You may get upset. Is that good for you? No. Is that good for the child? No. Then why create it? The marks did not create the feelings; you were its creator.

SO: But I would have thought it was just normal to be upset and feel sad.
SS: Once I get upset, my child also gets upset and demotivated. I expect him to do well in that demotivated state of mind. The energy that I am giving to those around me is not positive, and that's why I am not fulfilling my responsibility well. When my child scores less, my first responsibility is to first take charge of my mind. I have to remain composed so that I don't react impulsively. My next responsibility is to take care of his state of mind. After that I need to calmly explain that he needs to study responsibly and score well the next time.

SO: We usually do the opposite. We deplete their energy, lower their self-esteem, and belittle them. Today, suicide rate among children is on the rise.

SS: A big reason why a child commits suicide is that he is unable to face his parents after a failure. It is not because he failed, it is because he doesn't want to see his parents unhappy and he holds himself responsible for their unhappiness. The parents had conditioned and insisted that they would be happy only when he performed well.

SO: I thought it was my responsibility to ensure my child achieves his goal—whether in studies, sports, or whatever else. But have I been doing the opposite?

SS: Every individual's life is based on four aspects: physical health, intellectual development, emotional state of being and spiritual health. If I want to be successful and want my children to be successful in life—these four aspects need to be balanced.

As my responsibilities towards my child, I consider his academic and extracurricular performances, and I take care of his physical health. I might ensure the best home, the best food, the best comforts. For his social well-being, I expect him to have good friends. But how is my child feeling? We are not focused on that. Physically and academically he may be doing very well, but constant pressure, constant comparison with other children and the constant criticism he gets will deplete his emotional strength. As a parent, I need to ask myself whether I am fulfilling my responsibility. Tomorrow he could grow up to be an excellent doctor or lawyer, and be physically healthy.

But if he is emotionally weak, will he be successful? And if he is not resilient, can he be happy?

SO: What happens if he is not emotionally strong?
SS: If I am a good doctor, technically I am good. But if I am not emotionally strong, then I will get irritated very easily, I will react easily, I will not empathize with patients or colleagues. I will not get along with people because I am intolerant. Can I still call myself a good doctor?

We were all taught how to read, how to write, how to speak. No one taught us how to think.

SO: We knew only about IQ. EQ came into the picture much later.
SS: IQ is undoubtedly important, but so is emotional strength. An emotionally strong person can handle all struggles and challenges. With a strong IQ, we need emotional strength to be successful.

SO: Years ago, adults would slap children to discipline them. If they scored less marks, children were sacred to reveal it at home.
SS: Right. We need to ask ourselves whether we are fulfilling all our responsibilities correctly. It is not enough to fulfil just the one responsibility of getting them to perform well. What about our responsibility of making a child resilient? Life is going to present a lot of challenges. Today our child might be a topper, but will marks alone help him face life's challenges?

SO: He may be emotionally so weak that he cannot cope with several of life's situations.

SS: Exactly. If he has to face even a small failure, he will not be able to cope. What if he has to work with people and he cannot get along? We did not take care of that aspect. Why? Because we had not taken care of that aspect in our own lives. We ignored the importance of being emotionally healthy. We thought our responsibility is to take care of everything external, whether in our lives or the lives of those for whom we were responsible.

SO: Most men consider earning money to be their biggest responsibility.

SS: They need to check if their family is happy, if they believed happiness comes from outside.

SO: We provide toys, clothes, food, education. If they don't study, we blame their sanskaras, their school, or peer pressure. We keep blaming other people.

SS: Because we are not ready to take that responsibility. It's easy to earn and to send a child to the best school, to give the best food, the best home, and the best of everything. But it's a huge challenge to make a child emotionally strong.

SO: The most important thing to realise is that first I have to be emotionally strong. Let us do a meditation.

SS: While taking care of children, we always need to remember, we can send our child to the best school without having gone to school ourselves. We can ensure that our children eat well, even if we sleep on an empty stomach. But it is not possible to make our children happy without being happy ourselves. You cannot make your child emotionally strong without being emotionally strong yourself, so that's where the responsibility comes—to experience it yourself first.

Sit back and reflect on these thoughts:

Let us look at the journey of our life... aims, objectives, achievements... milestones to cover... that is my journey... Let me look at myself on the journey... the traveller with the changed consciousness.... Happiness is not at the destination... happiness is my state of being on the journey. I am happy... stable... in control... powerful while I am on the journey.... There are obstacles on the way... but my first responsibility is to take care of my state of being... of the way I respond. This is my responsibility. Om Shanti!

MANTRAS FOR HAPPINESS UNLIMITED

- Happiness is a state of being created while working towards the goal, not a feeling to be experienced after achieving the goal.
- If we believe that happiness is experienced after an achievement, we create stress, anger and fear while trying to achieve it.
- Before taking responsibility of those around us, we need to take responsibility for our own thinking and feelings. When we are happy and then take care of others, they will be happy.
- We cannot make our child emotionally strong without being emotionally strong ourselves.

CHAPTER THREE

SELF-CARE ISN'T SELFISH

SO: My friends mentioned something called the u-stress, which is good stress. They say we need that kind of stress. One of them said he actually waits till he is stressed and is short of time, because then he performs his best.
SS: It's a belief system. We hear people say—'Unless there is stress, I will not perform. If there is no stress I become passive and laid-back.' They call it the drive to perform, to achieve. So we need to ask ourselves if it is true. What is stress and how do I feel when I experience it? Suppose I suddenly develop a problem in my knee and it starts paining. I continue walking but do I feel as normal as I felt earlier?

SO: No, there is pain now.
SS: It's going to be uncomfortable. However, I say this is okay,

or even accept it as a natural part of ageing. I keep walking and because I am not treating it or taking care of it, the pain is constantly there and at times gets aggravated. I am still managing my life, though. If for some reason I need to run, will I be able to run with that pain? No.

It's the same with stress. Stress is in my mind; it is a little pain in the way I feel. How do I feel when I experience stress? Even if I am not able to check at an emotional level, let's just check the physical or bodily parameters—my heartbeat increases and so does my pulse rate, at times my mouth goes dry, I get an uncomfortable feeling in the stomach, my head feels heavy, and so on. This means the state of mind has already taken a toll on the body, and it is a much later stage. Some students fall ill on the day of their exams, with fever or nausea. Some people start sweating or their mouth goes dry before speaking in public. This is the effect of the mind on the body.

SO: I thought it was normal. The first time I faced a camera, my mouth went dry.
SS: Could you perform well?

SO: Not at all.
SS: Let's say a child has to appear for an exam. Exam is a target and a pressure. If he creates anxiety, can he perform better? When we used to give our exams and later evaluate the performance, we would find instances where we knew an answer but made a mistake. We referred to them as 'careless mistakes'. I know the answer but I have written something else.

This happens because there is not enough clarity, which is a state brought about by the presence of anxiety.

It's not carelessness. It has happened because I did not take care of my mind. So, there is lack of clarity, poor decision-making power, performance is affected, hands tremble, and speed of writing slows down. I may not even finish answering all the questions.

SO: So why do people say they work best when they are stressed or when a deadline is looming?
SS: Deadline means there is a target, and target could be a pressure. Target means I have to do this by this time. If there is no target, I may take six days to complete the same task. The minute you set a target, I start working faster. Now, while I am working faster, what will happen if I start creating thoughts along these lines—'How will I finish it by tomorrow evening? If I don't complete it, what will the consequence be? Will I lose my job? Will my boss hold it against me? What if someone else finishes it before I do? They will stand a better chance for promotion. My career will suffer...'

I am still performing, I am still working, but these thoughts are on my mind. What is going on in the mind is stress. This negativity is stress, and it is creating an uncomfortable feeling. The target is fine. Two people are given the same target: they have to finish this job by tomorrow evening, both are set to achieve it and they will. This means both will reach the destination, but their journey will be different. The other person may think 'Yes, I have to achieve this by tomorrow evening. I will focus on it and I am going to complete it'.

So, he reaches the destination with stability, whereas I reach there stressed. The end result is externally the same, for both of us have performed, but internally I am totally fatigued. I can conveniently blame pressure, and not realise that it is my own creation in the face of pressure.

Stress in science has a simple formula:

$$stress = pressure \div resilience$$

Pressure, the numerator here, includes what's coming from outside: targets, exams, relationships, situations, traffic jams, deadlines, etc. Resilience is my inner strength to face that pressure.

Consider metal sheets used in industrial applications. Different metal sheets are subjected to the same amount of pressure, but the stress factor of every metal is different, because every metal sheet's power to face that pressure is different.

Today, in the formula *stress = pressure ÷ resilience*, we have conveniently ignored the denominator and embraced the conditioning of stress = *pressure*.

The denominator is ignored because I am not ready to take responsibility for my inner strength. Hence, for me *stress = pressure*. So I say, if I have an exam, obviously I will get tensed. If my boss is very tough, obviously my workplace is going to be a challenge for me.

SO: Do people like to be stressed? Why do we accept it easily?
SS: When I am not able to tackle it, I just say it's natural or inevitable.

SO: Does it take effort to not be stressed and be happy in a situation?

SS: Yes. Suppose you say something unpleasant to me. Getting hurt can be so easy for me.

SO: I tend to think it's so natural to blame others for how we feel.

SS: It's summer today; a couple of months later it will be winter. It gets chilly. Do you say it's natural to fall ill since the weather has changed? No. You use your woollen-wear and protect yourself.

We don't keep blaming the weather, do we? We protect ourselves. Things are going to happen outside but because we have not learnt the mechanism of protecting ourselves, we say it is natural to fall ill, natural to get hurt, natural to get stressed.

$$\text{stress} = \text{pressure} \div \text{resilience}$$

Spirituality focusses on the denominator, that is resilience. The pressure or the situation is not in my control. So the numerator is not in my control. In any situation we can attribute 10% to the numerator, but the remaining 90% depends on my power to cope. Because if there is no pressure, then there will be no stress, so we give 10% responsibility to the pressure. The remaining 90% is about the extent I take charge, of how I am going to handle that pressure.

SO: So, how I react to something is 90%. Suppose somebody damages my car—if it's an old car, I don't get very upset. But if it's a brand new car, I react.

SS: How you react is your choice. Someone has hit your car—

the situation was not in your control. Now, you have two ways to respond: 1) Get out of the car, create a scene, shout at him, hit him, abuse him, have him respond in the same manner, and have ten people participate in the scene, or 2) wish him good morning and a nice day.

SO: Another choice is to just smile and say it's okay. In any case the car is insured.
SS: Yes. More important is the insurance of the mind. You claim insurance and your car is repaired. But every time a situation arises, for the damage that gets done inside, where is the insurance and where are the repairs?

SO: I am more concerned that my car is damaged.
SS: The car is more important than my happiness as per my responsibility list, because I thought the car was my source of happiness. Only when I make my state of being as my priority, will I start taking care of myself. First check if you are fine, then check if everything outside of you is fine.

SO: If you don't help yourself, how can you help others? But isn't this being a bit selfish?
SS: If I don't take care of myself, can I help you? All my time and energy is spent in taking care of other people. As a result, today we are under stress, and so is our family. Earlier, depression was seen in fewer people, that too in those aged over 60 years. Today children are facing mental health issues and are frequenting counsellors and psychiatrists. If we were fulfilling our responsibilities, this wouldn't be the result.

SO: We blame others for being irresponsible, but we need to take responsibility for ourselves.
SS: First I have to be responsible. The ability to respond is responsibility. My ability to respond in every situation is response + ability = responsibility.

The irony is we are always trying to control what is not in our control, ignoring what is. We say, 'My mind is not in my control', but that is the only thing which obeys us.

Let's go back to the example of two cars bumping into each other. If you suggest to people that they let go of the incident and drive away, they might not agree. They strongly believe it is important to punish the person who was at fault. Even if you explain that it is emotionally damaging for themselves, they do not agree. They will be keen on taking action so that the other person realises his mistake.

SO: Only then he won't repeat the mistake. I am doing him a favour.
SS: Can you see that I am more interested in teaching others, rather than taking care of myself? Whether it's a small situation or a big one, I have a choice of how to respond. Let me just sit back and be aware in every situation. If I just say it's okay and move on, how will I feel on that day?

SO: I would feel nice about it.
SS: Because I have conserved energy and conquered my own weakness of reacting. This is to be experimented with.

SO: The other day somebody banged into my car. My driver wanted to take action but I asked him to keep quiet and ignore the incident. I realize I felt nice because I conquered my weakness that had been present for years.

SS: Also, you had the right thoughts at that moment, so you felt better. If you create a thought that it is okay, it is after all an accident, let me move on now, it's a positive thought. It creates a good feeling. But if you think, 'Why wasn't he careful while driving? Who gave him a driving license? Does he think he owns the road?'—how are you going to feel after that?

Our thoughts determine our feelings. After creating such disturbing thoughts, we reach our destination, maybe our workplace.

SO: For how long would this mood and agitation remain?

SS: Let's say I drive for 30 minutes to work. So, the mood will stay for that long. The unfortunate part is, within the next 30 minutes, there will be another situation. By that time my emotional immunity is already low. So the chances of me reacting has increased.

I reach my office and my receptionist is not at her desk. Yet another situation confronts me. I go to my desk and see that my desk is not cleaned properly. One more situation. My junior has not completed his work; it was supposed to be ready. So, situation after situation unfolds, and I keep reacting. I justify my reactions saying it is because of someone or something.

SO: Am I not right in blaming? I didn't do anything but things happened, so my reactions were natural.

SS: By reacting, you are wasting and depleting your energy. You are reducing your emotional strength. When you encounter the next situation, you will be weaker than before.

SO: Over a period it becomes a habit and it takes a toll on health?
SS: Today we say high blood pressure is natural because we say stress is natural, and the by-product of this stress will also be natural. So everything that was unnatural gets labelled as natural. Yet we say we want happiness.

SO: What is the meaning of 'unlimited'?
SS: That which is not dependent on any limited object, people or situation. It's a state of being which is unlimited, unconditional, and independent. It is free of dependencies and, therefore, free of the fear of failure. Whenever there is dependency on someone or something, the second thought instantly will be of fear—What if I don't get it? I immediately create fear, and as I create fear, happiness is gone.

You will find people fearing happiness too. If everyone is happy, someone at home might say 'Don't be so happy, you never know what's going to happen next.' People are even scared to be happy today.

SO: Everything is temporary.
SS: Because we have made it dependent on situations. Right now the situation is favourable, so you are happy. But you don't know what the next situation is going to bring. But if your happiness is independent of situations, you can be happy 24 x 7.

SO: You think we can be happy 24 x 7?

SS: It's possible and we can be, but first we have to take care of ourselves and take self-responsibility. If we make happiness dependent on outside factors, it becomes occasional. The more the situations become challenging, the more people's behaviours become unpredictable. It becomes a struggle and that is when we start accepting stress as natural, whereas it is happiness that is natural.

SO: Thank you so much for explaining how stress is not natural—happiness is. Could we do a brief meditation?

SS: Relax and reflect on these thoughts.

Let us sit back and be comfortable... I look at myself... I, the creator of every thought and feeling... There are pressures in life... targets to achieve... deadlines to meet... It's just a pressure... I am the one who is going to achieve the target... let me take care of myself as I work towards achieving the target... The quality of my thoughts and feelings as I move towards the target... any fear... any anxiety... any worry... let me first sit back and change the quality of the thought... I am a powerful being... I can achieve what I have decided... but I will first take care of myself... Nothing and no one can influence my state of being... It's totally in my control... I, the powerful being... protected and secure... now move towards my target. This is my journey, a journey of happiness. Om Shanti!

MANTRAS FOR HAPPINESS UNLIMITED

- Stress is a pain that comes to tell us we need to change something internally.
- Stress is our creation of negative thoughts, which has an effect on our efficiency, memory power, decision power and, hence, our performance.
- Stress has an impact on our physical and emotional well-being, and hence, any amount of stress is damaging.
- Targets, pressures, deadlines, exams, etc., are natural, but stress is our choice.
- Stress = pressure ÷ resilience. Resilience is inner strength. Our first responsibility in any situation is to first take charge of our state of mind because that is the only entity in our control.

CHAPTER FOUR

STOP 'WANTING' HAPPINESS, BE HAPPY

SO: I read an article in a newspaper; that said 'Peace feeds happiness. What comes first, peace or happiness? Can you be at peace if you are not happy? The answer to these questions depends on your idea of happiness, on whether you get happiness from external factors or from within'.

SS: Yes, we read and hear about it often, but what happens at the time of practical implementation? We read about the subject every day in the newspaper, in the spiritual literature section or in self-help books. Today the largest-selling books are on the topics of self-help and positive-thinking, motivation, self-development and spirituality. Seminars and workshops are organised. Yet, stress, anger and anxiety are on the rise. So unlimited happiness becomes a question mark—even though there is ample knowledge and realization, we are looking for happiness outside. This means we haven't internalised the knowledge. Instead, we are accepting stress as natural. So there is a wide gap between what I know, what I read, what I believe, and what I implement.

SO: Do we not believe in what we read?
SS: It's not become a part of our belief system yet. 'Stress is natural' is a belief system we have adopted right from our childhood. As a child, we had our parents asking, 'Aren't you tensed? You have an exam tomorrow. How can you be so relaxed?' The belief was further reinforced by society, which says 'Stress is obvious, with all the competition around you'. So this belief that we have lived with has become deep rooted.

Today if I read somewhere 'Happiness is your natural way of living, natural way of being, it's your choice,' it doesn't suddenly replace my old belief system. So I just read it and carry on with my life, believing stress is natural, not happiness. I say it doesn't work in daily life. This is how workshops, spirituality and religion get separated from my practical life. I go to a retreat, attend a management workshop or a spiritual programme, and listen to pure and powerful information. While I am listening, I absolutely agree with it. But when I come back, I am still my old self and say those things don't work here. I even say it was easy for those people to say what they did, but they are not living my circumstances.

We don't even try; we don't experiment with the right beliefs. We think transformation will happen automatically. Well, it won't. Whatever I have studied and whatever I have understood, I will have to put in a little effort at applying it. Now

I have understood that anger is unnatural, that it is a response I create. So when I come to my workplace or spend time with my family, I have to take care that I do not react angrily.

SO: I was restless by nature and wanted peace. I asked my Guru but she said, 'You often ask me about peace, but do you do any karmas of peace?' I could not relate to what she was saying. When I came out, somebody had parked his car in front of mine. I was so furious. I opened my car door and wanted to honk, but I remembered her words about doing karmas of peace.

SS: I want peace but I think it has to come from outside. Similarly, I want happiness, I want love, and so on. 'Want' means that someone, somewhere has to do something so that I will get it. On the other hand, spirituality teaches us that I am peace. I have to be at peace while I am doing everything. I am a blissful being. I am a love-full being.

SO: But if I am, then why do I want?
SS: Because I have forgotten that I am. It's like the keys in your pocket or the spectacles on your head. You have them with you but sometimes you look for them and even get others to join you in that search.

SO: How do I realize or understand that I am peace? How to prove it?
SS: By experimenting. Everything is a belief; we experiment with it, and if we get the result, we take it as the truth. We hear, 'Keep searching for peace, for that's the purpose of life'.

If the purpose of life is to keep searching for peace, then when will we find it?

But now we understand peace is our nature. Let me experiment—I am a peaceful being. Now I will use this awareness in every act, with every person. In every interaction today, I will only remember that I am the one who is doing it. Think of a doctor. He knows he is a doctor, so if someone meets with an accident while he is around, he will immediately get into the healing job. But if the doctor forgets that he is a doctor, even if people around him are bleeding, he won't do anything, because he has forgotten he is a doctor. So healing won't come into action. But the minute he remembers who he is, he will start healing.

So it's about awareness That. I am a peaceful being was forgotten. And because it was forgotten, I was looking for peace outside. Now let's try a new belief system that we are peace. Try it—it's still not the truth; it's only a belief. Just experiment with it. If we get the result, then it is the truth.

SO: How to experiment?
SS: When I go back to work today and if there is a situation, I just remind myself that I am a peaceful being and then act.

SO: Is it like a mantra that 'I am a peaceful being, I am a peaceful being'? If someone says something unpleasant, I may get angry. And later I remember the mantra again, that I am a peaceful being.
SS: It's not a mantra; it's a conviction. I am telling

41

myself who I am, and preparing myself. Everything that I do will be out of this consciousness. This is who I am. It's simple.

Let us say there is a space in the mind. I believe it is empty and say I want happiness, I want peace and I want love. I go to everyone expecting them to fill that space. I say, 'Please do this so that I will be happy. Please talk to me nicely so that I will be peaceful.' This is one way of living, one belief system. The other belief system is that the space is full of peace, but now I have to go through the whole day taking care not to spill out that peace. That is it. It is full and I have to take care of it. This is the journey, this is what *Awakening with Brahma Kumaris* is all about. It is about understanding that I am peaceful. I just have to remember that while talking to you I should not spill it out.

SO: I am peaceful. The moment I am not peaceful, does it spill out?
SS: One way is: I do this so that I will be happy. The other way is: I am happy and now I will do this.

SO: I am happy and I will try to make you happy too.
SS: I don't know whether I will be able to make other people happy; that is another belief we need to evaluate.

SO: What I meant is, when you are around a happy person, you also feel happy because the atmosphere is happy.
SS: True, but someone can be around a happy person and still be very sad, unless they take charge of their thoughts and feelings. This again is an incorrect, deep belief that we can

make others happy. No one can make someone happy, unless they want to be happy themselves.

SO: Then no one can make us sad too.
SS: Absolutely, I am not dependent on other people for my emotions and my feelings. But the most widespread, incorrect belief system is—My happiness is dependent on other people.

SO: When we love someone we say, 'This person makes me happy'.
SS: When I am with this person, I have nice thoughts. So I tell myself I am happy when I am with this person. And then I tell myself, 'This person makes me happy'.

This is how we also become dependent on objects—whether a car or a piece of jewellery—to create similar kinds of thoughts. We use these as stimulus to create a particular kind of thought. Between the stimulus and the response is my freedom to choose a response. Today if you talk to me nicely, I am happy. Tomorrow if you do something that according to me is not right, I can be hurt. But you are still the same.

SO: I was different yesterday. I was speaking to you nicely. My behaviour is changed.
SS: So my response is dependent on your behaviour. Are you always going to behave the way I want you to?

SO: No, I am going to be in different moods on different days, at different times.
SS: Are you wrong?

SO: It is normal.
SS: Are you wrong?

SO: I am right.
SS: According to?

SO: Myself.
SS: But according to me, you are wrong. So, I have conditioned myself to believe this is right and this is wrong. I want people to be right so that I will be happy.

SO: So you try to control my behaviour, always being nice to you?
SS: Yes, because then I will be happy.

SO: So are you controlling me?
SS: Yes, I am controlling you, and that's what we are doing everyday with people. We are doing that with our children, with everyone around us. We want them to be or do or perform or behave in a particular manner, because that will make us happy.

I feel what I think is right and the other person is wrong, so my happiness becomes dependent on them.

SO: What are relationships for? We depend on friends. If I am in a problem, I need help.
SS: That's fine. But my pain or happiness being dependent on the other person's behaviour is not right. Let's say I expected you to call me up last evening. If you didn't call

me, I am hurt. Why? Since my happiness was dependent on your behaviour.

SO: I still feel that is natural. If my wife calls and talks to other people except me, I feel hurt.
SS: You have a choice.

SO: This is what I want to learn.
SS: You have a choice. She did not call me, though I thought she should have. I could still be stable by creating different thoughts, that she was busy, or that she did not feel like talking to me at that time.

SO: I got the answer. My friend reached his home and it was locked. He would have broken the lock in anger, but he had returned from a spiritual retreat. So he went to his daughter's house and picked the spare key. Just as he went inside, his wife returned. He asked her where she had been. She had been to the market and had tried to contact him, but his phone was switched off. He realised that he had switched it off during the retreat. This meant that she was right and so was he.
SS: Absolutely. Everyone is always right. It's not important whether they are right or wrong. First of all, I have to be right—not do right but BE right. This means I first take care of myself. This will only happen when I gradually bring myself out of this mental conditioning that my state of mind is dependent on other people.

We hold so many people responsible for our pain. So we are telling ourselves it's their fault, and I am fine the way I am.

I have to understand that people are doing what they are doing; they could be cheating on me, but my pain is my creation. Even if you have cheated me as a business partner, the hurt, the resentment and the hatred that I feel are my creation. You cheated me financially and ethically, and that's where your power ends. That's where the power of anybody outside ends, whether it's a business partner, a spouse, or a child.

Our thoughts, feelings and responses are OUR choice.

SO: But it troubles me inside. Why can't I retaliate?
SS: Let's say your business partner cheated and you parted ways. Now you decide to do the same business that he is doing, with the thought, 'I want to enter the market as his competitor. I want to take my revenge. I believe I am right'. You want to start a business with vengeance. Is this the kind of energy to bring into your work? Is this thought process right?

How you think and feel is your choice. Whether you create hurt and for how long you will remain hurt is also your choice. Whether you live with your pain for 10 minutes, 10 days, or 10 years is your choice. You can sit back, think of the situation, and relive the pain again and again, even years after it happened. Who is the creator of these emotions? It's you. In the same situation, different people will create different responses. This has to be experimented with at every step.

SO: If my wife didn't call me when I expected her to, she had reasons. But my mind goes on thinking.
SS: Whose mind is it?

SO: My mind.
SS: Who is creating the thoughts?

SO: The mind, not me.
SS: Whose mind is it?

SO: My mind.
SS: So who is creating the thoughts?

SO: I will say my mind is creating the thoughts.
SS: But it's my mind, so who is creating the thoughts? I am. Look at yourself creating those thoughts; 'She should have called me. I was waiting for her call.' Now you sit back and just change your thoughts gradually to 'She didn't feel like talking to me at that time. It was her choice.'

SO: But my mind says she should be happy to speak to me.
SS: Yes, because I like people to be dependent on me. I am dependent too. It's this control that gives me power. I am empty inside and I love this idea of people being dependent on me. I think I am more powerful because people are dependent on me for feeling good. Because I am dependent on other people, I feel other people should also be dependent on me for feeling happy. So I think, 'How could she be happy without talking to me, when I am not happy without talking to her?'

We are trapped, and we are trapping other people into being dependent on us. All this is happening in the name of love, respect and trust, which are supposed to be unconditional.

SO: Let us have a minute of meditation.

SS: Relax and reflect on these thoughts.

Let me look at the people around me... my friends, my family, and my immediate relationships... Everyone around me at home and at work... doing and being exactly the way they think is right... Their behaviour and their words are the stimulus that's coming from outside... I, the being, choose my response... My response is not automated... it's not in their control... it's my choice... Let me look at myself with them... they are behaving in a manner that I think is not right.... Now let me look at myself... in control... in charge... not of them... not of the situation... but of my state of mind... I am creating the right thought at the right time... I am the master... an independent... powerful being. Om Shanti!

MANTRAS FOR HAPPINESS UNLIMITED

- Our belief systems decide our way of living. We need to experiment with what we learn, in order to change incorrect belief systems.
- Experiment with this belief: 'I don't want peace. I am peace. Now I will be at peace and do things outside.'
- Try a new belief system. When you experience the result, it becomes the truth.
- Every act we do, let's do it with the awareness that we are peaceful beings.
- Unlimited Happiness is not dependent on people, objects or situations. No one can make us happy and we can't make others happy, till they want it themselves.
- No one is responsible for our hurt, pain, fear, or anger. It is our own creation in response to their behaviour, and we have another choice—the choice to be happy.

CHAPTER FIVE

WHO CONTROLS YOUR EMOTIONAL BUTTONS?

SO: I am in charge of my emotions. I cannot play blame anymore. But how do I avoid reacting when people say something unpleasant?

SS: I am not saying that we do not respond. If you are saying something to me, I am not supposed to sit like a stone wall with no thoughts, feelings or emotions. That's not right. The question is—what thoughts, what feelings, what emotions? It's not that I either react or don't respond at all. Reaction means an automated response. Sometimes we regret our reactions, and then say sorry to people.

SO: I regret my words or action so often.
SS: What do we regret?

SO: Unnecessary retaliations.
SS: We regret our own reactions. You behave in a certain manner and I react, and then I have to come back and apologize.

SO: Because I overreacted in response to how the other person behaved.
SS: It's not about the magnitude. It is about not being comfortable with the way I reacted. Normally we measure, like you said 'overreacted'. This means we are always measuring our reactions with reference to the other person's behaviour. If you shout at me, I shout louder. We are always doing it with reference to other people. My personality should be mine, my responses should be mine, and my way of talking should be mine, irrespective of the other person. If I keep changing with reference to everyone I meet, there will be nothing left in me that is of my own.

SO: Somebody passes by without greeting me. I think 'He didn't wish me; why should I?'
SS: Let's say courtesy is your quality. Being nice and friendly comes naturally to you; it's your personality. You are walking along a corridor, and you are about to wish me 'good morning'. However, I just ignore and move past you. I am cold at this particular moment, for whatever reason—may be my nature or my present mood. I am not courteous, but because of me, you give up your quality as well.

Next, you meet someone else who behaves differently, and then you give up another quality. Then meet someone who shouts at you and you give up your politeness. Gradually we absorb people's negativity and give up our qualities.

SO: How does one stick to one's quality?
SS: Remembering this is my personality. And this personality is going to be out there interacting, irrespective of their behaviors. So we can take even one quality, let's say being courteous, and stick to it.

SO: My mantra for today: I will be courteous, no matter what.
SS: As simple as that. That's what I have to tell myself. My nature remains my nature, irrespective of external stimulus.

SO: We can observe a fast even on days when we have to go to a restaurant or a party. The same way, we can be courteous, irrespective of the situation.
SS: Absolutely. Take only one quality today—being courteous, being humble or politeness is your quality. Don't let it change.

SO: People's behaviour changes with different people. Why does it happen?
SS: We keep changing our personality so many times during the day that we are not even aware of what our true nature is. To our spouse, we may say 'Bring the glass of water,' and to someone else we may say 'May I have a glass of water, please?' Which of these is my original nature? It's just that when we are with our spouse, we do not take the responsibility of pleasing them; we take them for granted.

SO: Which one is artificial?
SS: I have to ask myself.

SO: Will my spouse feel nice if I speak courteously to her?
SS: More important is—you will feel nice if you speak that way to her. Our behaviour is not for other people; it is primarily for us. Will I speak sweetly to you so that you are happy? No, I will speak sweetly because it makes me feel nice.

SO: I have seen people do so many things only to please the outside world.
SS: It is good. But let's add one criterion here: taking care of myself first and doing for others what I feel comfortable doing.

There are a lot of people who are doing things for others. But when they do not get something in return, they get upset. Should we be doing it because we want something in return?

SO: What if we get only criticism in return?
SS: First of all, I need to check how I was feeling while doing it. If I felt nice, that's sufficient. Now if I get criticism, I just check whether the criticism is valid.

SO: I got an email from my niece, in which she recounted two incidents when I was rude to her, making her unhappy. My justification was 'It was because I was tired'. But I truly was rude.
SS: You can apologise now. But that will only happen because you have started checking yourself. We like to justify our

inadequacies and hide our weaknesses. If we start justifying rudeness, the list can be long.

SO: I am not doing anything. I blame my mind as it plays games with me.
SS: My mind is mine. It's my responsibility. We speak about our mind as if it is separate from us. We are not ready to take responsibility of our mind; we say it is not in our control. It's like a parent who has given up on their child. Someone comes and says 'Your child is not behaving properly,' and you reply 'Sorry, my child is not in my control; please take care of my child'.

Because my mind is not in my control, I try to control your mind. If you say something and I am not able to control my mind, I try to control you. I ask you, 'Is this the way you should speak?', because I am not asking my mind, 'Is this the way I should think?' So I focus on teaching you how to speak because if you speak nicely, my mind is comfortable.

Let's see how we want to think, feel and be in every relationship.

SO: How I want to think, feel and be in every relationship!
SS: Let's not concentrate on them. Our attention is usually about making other people happy.

SO: That is tiring.
SS: But don't you think we are doing it every day? I want my family to be happy, colleagues to be happy, friends to be happy. I am doing a lot for them. It's a genuine effort. I want

people to be happy with me, because I believe that when they are happy, I will be happy.

SO: Either this, or we show no interest in anyone's happiness. How do I strike a balance?
SS: In India, when a married girl comes to her husband's home, in many families she is expected to quit her job. I have met a lot of such women who have given up their careers. But they say the husband's family is still not happy with them. They get frustrated. As a newly married young girl, when she came into the family, it was projected that the family would be happy when she quit her job. To keep them happy she quit her job, but on the inside, she was not happy about the decision.

SO: Maybe they are unhappy for some other reason.
SS: No other reason. She has done this to make them happy, but she has been unhappy from the day she quit her job. She is staying in the same house for 20 years; she chose not to work, but chose it for their happiness. It's not a choice that she made for herself. She did what they wanted, but she is not happy doing it. So what's her message or energy to them for last years? 'I am unhappy, I am unhappy because of you.' So, how can that family be happy?

SO: So they can't be happy just because she is sending them constant negative energy?
SS: This is where the secret lies. I cannot make other people happy by doing 'anything' for them. If I choose to do something,

I have to be happy first while doing it. Otherwise, I shouldn't do it at all.

SO: But aren't certain things to be done whether you are or you are not happy?
SS: You will do the act, but you will not give it the right energy. Suppose I give you a gift because it is my duty to give it. But internally I am upset and disinterested. So you won't be happy, maybe you won't even look at the gift, because you are going to get the energy of the giver. So I did this for you, but what was my energy? Relationships are not actions. Relationships are energies that we exchange while doing those actions. So if something is my duty, I should first convince my mind why I am doing it. I tell the mind, 'I am choosing to do this. I am doing it because these people matter to me.' Create the right thought and the right energy first before doing something, otherwise it is best to not even do it.

SO: What is the meaning of duty?
SS: Responsibility. We are living with people, and they have certain expectations of how they want me to be and what they want me to do. I consider it my responsibility and my pure desire to make them happy, so I do what they want me to do. But if I do it unhappily, it will not get me the desired results. Moreover, because I am doing it for them, very soon I will be expecting them to do something for me.

SO: It's difficult to internalize this.
SS: That's because our focus is all on the 'doing'. Look at the

priorities through the day—I have to DO this, I have to DO that. The focus has rarely been—I have to BE like this.

SO: Children say—I have to do so much homework. Isn't that correct?
SS: Yes, they have to do it. Care has to be on how they feel while doing it. They need to be calm, peaceful, happy, and then do it. Let's say I have to run from here to there. I have to be healthy to do it. If I am not healthy and I try to run, the journey will be tiresome, painful and a struggle. Likewise, for everything I do the whole day, for my entire life, I need to be emotionally healthy. Only then what I do will be beautiful.

SO: How can I be emotionally healthy?
SS: That's an important aspect of life which we have taken for granted. We thought it will happen on its own. Or we even thought other people will take care of it for us—that we are all supposed to make each other happy.

SO: I knew some people who were fed up of their parents and waited to get married. But they were not happy after marriage either. How can one to be emotionally balanced and stable always?
SS: There are people who are not happy in their marriages and looking for relationships outside their marriage.

SO: They break that as well and go for yet another marriage.
SS: Because we thought happiness has to come from the other person. So we kept searching.

SO: We can conclude that happiness cannot come from outside. We went to spiritual centres, did social work, went shopping, watched movies… as we wanted to be happy.

SS: Whenever I distract my mind, what happens? When I am watching a television show or a movie, whatever was going on in my mind is put off for some time. Suppose you have a toothache and you start watching a movie; very soon you will forget the toothache. But when you switch off the TV, the pain seems to start again. What happened? Does it mean that the tooth was healed and now it's hurting again? No, the pain was always there but the mind was distracted. My tooth is aching and I am aware of the pain. Who is aware of the pain? The mind is. Then I divert my mind to something else—a conversation, shopping trip, or television programme. I feel the pain is gone but it is not—it's just that I am not aware of the pain. When the TV is switched off, I can feel the pain again.

This is for physical pain, but the same is true for an emotional pain. The whole day was tough, I created a lot of stress and anxiety; then I say 'let's go for a movie,' 'let's go on a holiday,' 'let's take a break from here and go away for 15 days.'

SO: Is it escapism?

SS: It's just that we are trying to take the mind away from there.

SO: Shall we call it temporary happiness?

SS: Not happiness, it's a temporary distraction of the mind from the truth. It's not happiness because we are coming back to it after sometime. We can call it happiness if it was healed. The tooth was not healed; it was just that we were not aware of the pain.

SO: So why do we go for holidays, picnics, movies and all that?
SS: For a change, for entertainment, it's different from the routine.

SO: Please tell us a little about meditation, to experience happiness 24x7, without being dependent on others for it.
SS: Let's just be aware of our thoughts, and let's not try and deviate our mind to something else in the pursuit of happiness. I am only suppressing the conscious mind by getting distracted, thinking it brings happiness. The minute the distraction is removed, the conscious mind is back there, and probably with more pain. I need to take charge. This is not the solution, I am shying away from the problem. But for how long can I run away? How long can I be on a holiday? Finally, I am going to be back.

Relax and reflect on these thoughts. Meditate.

Let's look at ourselves... tomorrow at work... whatever the situation may be... I am not blaming anyone... I am not going to hold anyone responsible for how I feel... because I understand that I am the creator... just when my mind is about to say it's because of them... let me just stop and look at myself... do I have a choice to respond in another way... what's my nature, my personality... let it not get influenced by the behaviours and personalities of others... I am the radiator of my qualities irrespective of whatever happens around me.... This is self-responsibility.... Om Shanti!

MANTRAS FOR HAPPINESS UNLIMITED

- Our responses to people should be based on our personality, not on their behaviour.
- The way we think and behave is not for other people. It is first for ourselves because we are the first ones to experience it.
- Let us take charge of our mind instead of trying to control others, believing that if they change, our mind will be in control.
- Let us choose how we want to think, feel and be in every relationship. We have always tried to make others happy because we thought when they would be happy, we will be happy too.
- When we do something for others, let us first understand that we chose to do it because they matter to us and we are doing it for ourselves. Only then will we be happy.
- Diverting the mind from problems by watching television, going shopping and other distractions is only a temporary deviation from the pain. It is not happiness, because the healing has not happened.

CHAPTER SIX

ONE UNDERSTANDING THAT ENDS DISAPPOINTMENTS

SO: I read that peace and happiness almost go hand in hand. The writer says there is peace in the smile of a child, in the tender touch of one's mother; it has got nothing to do with God or religion but everything to do with the state of one's mind.

SS: Absolutely. In both instances, the author is talking about vibrations of the being. The smile of a child emanates vibrations of purity and innocence, and the touch of the mother has vibrations of love and unconditional acceptance. When we experience these gestures, more than the act, it is the vibration in the energy that we experience. That's why there is peace. And wherever there is peace, there will be happiness.

SO: For a mother and a child it is so natural. For others we need to make an effort.

SS: That's what it's all about. About making it natural. Effort happens when you are trying to do it for the other person, while natural is when you are just being yourself. If I am trying to do things according to what I think will make you happy, then it is an effort. But if I am just being myself, then it's natural.

SO: Being myself or being natural is peace, love and happiness, is it?

SS: Yes. I need to be aware that these are my natural qualities. These are not qualities I acquire by doing something. It's my natural personality; they are my natural *sanskars*. It's my original state of being; I just have to remember it and let them flow—not look for them outside.

SO: People say, 'I am a Leo,' 'I am a Taurus,' 'I am a so-and-so.' That is why I am a short-tempered. We attributed behaviors to sun signs and that is wrong.

SS: There's a very beautiful word in Hindi—*sanskars*. It means personality traits. Every being carries *five types of sanskars*. It's important to understand the being, because it is a package made of these five types of *sanskars*. The first set of *sanskars* we get from the family. We are in the vicinity of family members, so their energy automatically influences us. The second set of *sanskars* comes from my environment, country, religion, city, school and friends. We have always heard—you will be coloured by the company you keep. The environment and people around you, the energy around you, the belief systems around you, create *sanskars*.

The third type of *sanskars* are from our past. When I understand that I am an eternal spiritual being—I just change costumes and my soul journey is through different costumes. There are certain *sanskars* I have created in my past costumes. Today I am in this costume, coming into action, they are all creating an impression, which is a *sanskar*. When it is time to leave this body, *sanskars* don't get erased, they are carried forward into the next birth. It's like a recording of songs on the CD that was created. When you insert that CD into another player, those songs are still there.

SO: Let's forget about past life since we don't know how many of us believe in it.
SS: It's not about belief. It's because we don't understand it that we have conflicting views. The biggest conflict today in a family is that parents expect their children to be the same. They ask—'I have given the same upbringing to both my children, why are they so different?' Parents are same, family is same, environment is same, so they expect *sanskars* of their children to be the same. Yet, two children can be twins, born under the same zodiac sign too—same date and same place. They may go to the same school, grow in the same environment, but their personalities will be different. Because few years ago when they were in two different costumes, they were not in the same family, not in the same country, and not in the same environment. They have had a different past, and they are carrying their pasts. We cannot ignore past life's *sanskars* because they are dominant factors in

determining the present. We fail to understand people because we are only seeing them in their present costume. We are unable to see that they are carrying a past.

SO: It's a wise way for parents to understand children.
SS: Parents compare and tell a child, 'Look at your brother, you should be like him.' We don't understand that they are two different personalities like two CDs having two different recordings. They have now come to our house and we are trying to make one similar to the other.

SO: I have heard mothers doubting if their child actually belongs to them.
SS: That mother fails to understand where her child has got *sanskars* from, as she hasn't given them to the child. It's tough for the child too, because even he doesn't know why he has these *sanskars*. For example, a child could have a *sanskar* of stealing. He comes from a wealthy family and has all comforts at home. But he steals another child's pencil at school. It comes instinctively to him, he doesn't intend or plan to steal it. This is because the being, the spiritual energy, the soul has carried such a *sanskar*. When we are unaware, our *sanskars* come into play automatically.

SO: It's difficult to reach this level of awareness. Often there is such a small gap between a stimulus and my response.
SS: It comes with attention and practice. Years back, if somebody's mobile phone rang while I was conducting a programme, I would get disturbed.

SO: Earlier you were disturbed, later you remained stable. Does it happen in stages?

SS: Some people say it's going to take years. No, it doesn't take years. It's just one thought of awareness—otherwise I can get irritated by a ringing mobile phone for a lifetime. We can live our lives getting irritated by mobiles ringing around us.

SO: What does 'one thought of awareness' mean?

SS: One thought is—'How can I allow a trivial thing like a ringtone to disturb my mind?' This is just one thought.

I don't think about that person whose phone is ringing. It is not the ringtone that disturbs us, but it is the thought we create after listening to the ringtone—"Why did they not switch off their mobiles? Don't they know that they are in a public programme?" So it's not the ringtone that irritates me. It's the thoughts that I create in response to the ringtone that irritate me. The ringtone is just a trigger. I have to realize what is disturbing me. It is my own thoughts. My thought is that they should have switched off the phone. Now I change my thought—'Whether they want to switch it off or not is their choice, and I respect their choice.'

SO: I would get disturbed even if somebody walked in front of me while I was shooting my scene. Now I see so many people moving around, and am learning to accept it.

SS: Now this is where we are creating the fourth type of *sanskar*. Getting irritated was one of the past *sanskars*, maybe from past birth, or from the current environment. With awareness, we can change our *sanskar*. We are creating *sanskars* with our own will power. Again, we cannot keep blame and say 'I can't help it, this must be a past *sanskar*.' It's all about awareness and then change.

SO: Does awareness bring will power?
SS: Yes. I use will power to create a new *sanskar*. Every time I say 'This is because of you' or 'I am getting irritated because of this', I imply that I am not powerful and others can overpower me. Will power means I have the power to choose, to think, to be and to do what I want. Every time I use that power, it's will power. Many times we feel we don't have will power. Everyone has the same amount of will power. It just depends on how much we are using it. We disempower ourselves by not using our will power.

SO: Someone I know took just 2 days to quit his drinking habit of 30 years. If I have the same amount of will power as him, why am I unable to see that I too have will power?
SS: It's simple: I am not using it. Any human quality is handy only if it is being used.

SO: What if I don't know how to see or use a particular quality?
SS: That's why we are learning. It's that area of life we are now focusing attention on. By saying we don't have time for spirituality, or we don't have time to meditate, we choose not to use the powers that we have. It's like I have a whole lot of property in my locker but I refuse to open it and use it. Instead I go around begging people for love, peace and

happiness because I am not using that time to go to my own locker and fetch them from there.

SO: So your locker is meditation is it?
SS: It's here in the mind. The key is with us, and only we know how to open it.

SO: Is there no need to go to anyone to get my locker opened, or to develop my powers?
SS: Somebody can guide us how to open it, but no one else can open it for us. No one can activate our will power for us. They can only help us realize that we have it. A simple example is when we want to give up an addiction. Someone may want to give up alcohol or cut down TV time or social media. We create a powerful positive thought:

'Today I will watch TV only for an hour.' We are aware of this positive thought we create, but we are not aware of so many negative thoughts that follow—'It is difficult for me... I love watching TV... I have tried many times but always failed... It's my habit... Can't go in one day... Obviously it will take time.'

Now, we created one positive thought to empower ourselves, and then followed it with several negative thoughts, which will disempower us. Once we decide to do something, we just need to create one single thought and start working on it.

SO: If we have equal will power, how can few people give up addictions sooner than others?
SS: Everyone has equal will power, because everyone is a powerful being. Realizing my own will power depends on

my awareness that I am powerful, and how much I use it. Of course, people around me also make a difference.

We are largely responsible for reducing the will power of people around us, especially of children. If your child spends hours on social media, you may ask him to cut it down to an hour. Your words are affirmative, but your thoughts are of doubt and failure, about his giving up the social-media addiction.

SO: Internally I am so sure that my child will not be able to do it.
SS: Every thought that I create about my child is energy that I am showing or radiating to him.

SO: But why should the child get disturbed by the energy of his parent?
SS: We get influenced by the thoughts, words and actions of other people. We have to be very strong and protected to not get affected. That can happen if we practice not getting influenced by the energies around us. Right now, we are quite vulnerable. Everything happening around us creates an impact. If a child is trying to achieve something, we should not create a single thought of doubt or fear. Otherwise we disempower the child. Let us create only powerful thoughts—'You can do it; we have faith in you.' Even if the child does not have the power, he will get empowered.

Today corporate sector is trying to motivate the workforce. Motivation cannot happen with words. If your subordinate comes in late every day, you motivate him by saying 'I am sure you will be punctual henceforth.' But your thinking is 'I know him. He will not come on time. He will never change.'

Our thoughts and words are different. When we say we are family and we are friends and we are there for each other, let it not be just in words. There should be harmony between thoughts and words. That's the simplest thing to take care in relationships. When there is a difference, there is also a conflict in our energy, which the opposite person receives. Remember, thought energy travels faster.

SO: We say, 'Wow, nice shirt', though we think 'He doesn't have good taste'.
SS: Why do we say he is wearing a nice shirt?

SO: A lot of people talk like that. We pick it up from everyone around us.
SS: But why do I say to you that your shirt is very nice?

SO: To please people.
SS: To please people. This is extremely important. We are saying things just to make people happy. But happiness is not words; happiness is energy, vibrations, feelings. I am sending a word out by paying a compliment to your shirt, and I am also sending thoughts that it is a horrible shirt, horrible choice, no taste at all.

So what's the total energy that comes to you? Vibration reaches faster and is much more powerful than our words.

SO: Will he know that I did not like his shirt?
SS: He won't be able to catch your thoughts. We can't catch people's thoughts. The mind needs to be extremely silent to be able to catch people's thoughts, but we can catch feelings and vibrations. That is why after meeting certain people, despite having a polite conversation we say, 'I don't think they meant what they said. I didn't feel nice meeting them.' The foundation of this relationship is false, so it's no relationship at all. If I send this conflicting energy to you, you will doubt my intentions and then you will always doubt my intention. There is no trust. One misunderstanding is enough to crash that relationship because there hardly was a foundation. We need to ask ourselves what we are doing.

One option is this: I don't say that you are wearing a nice shirt, if I am not convinced that it is nice. If I don't feel it's nice, I shouldn't say it's nice. This is integrity. If at all I still want to say it's nice, first let 'me' understand that it's nice, by creating a thought—'I might not like a white shirt, but that's just my choice. His choice is nice for him.' Create this thought and then say it. I need to keep working on myself till my thought and words are in harmony, and then I need to communicate. That is clean communication.

SO: If I tell him his shirt is nice when I actually do not mean it, what happens to me?
SS: I am cheating myself. I am not honest to myself. I don't do what I think. There is disharmony between my thoughts, words and actions. I think something else, I say something else, and I do something else. This disharmony flows into in

other aspects. I will think I have to do this, but my words and actions will not follow. So my will power reduces. That is why our will power is low today.

SO: We understood the four types of *sanskars*. Which is the fifth type?
SS: The fifth *sanskars* are the original *sanskars*. When I understand my original *sanskars*, I can easily take care of the first four. My past birth *sanskars* are not in my control; *sanskars* from family are not in my control, *sanskars* from the environment are not in my control. Will power is in my control. I can create new *sanskars* through my will power. But even will power gets activated only when I understand my original *sanskars*, my original nature, and that's the original nature of every human soul on this planet.

Every being is originally pure, affectionate, peaceful, blissful and powerful. Every being has this nature and we are looking for it outside, only because we have forgotten that this is our own nature. Spirituality shifts our belief from, 'I want happiness and peace', to the truth that 'I am a peaceful being. I am a blissful being. I am a powerful being.' And then my whole perspective will change. If I understand that I am peace, I become a giver. It ends my seeking for happiness, asking for love. I start sharing peace, love and happiness with everyone. It automatically flows from me to people around me.

Like when we are stressed, we don't have to consciously give it to others; anyone coming into our energy field automatically receives it and are influenced by us. Similarly, by being in our natural state of peace and happiness, we don't have to give it to others, it will naturally radiate and will be felt by family and friends. Energy is like an infection—we catch it from the people around us.

SO: I am peace. I am love. I am knowledge. I am bliss.

MANTRAS FOR HAPPINESS UNLIMITED

- Our personality is a combination of five types of *sanskars*—personality traits.
- We get one set of *sanskars* from our parents and other family members. We call these hereditary *sanskars* because we are within the influence of their vibrations.
- There are *sanskars* we create because of our environment: our nationality, religion, culture and friends.
- A very important set of *sanskars* are those that we carry from our past birth. The soul carries personality traits created in one costume, into the next costume.
- We create the fourth type of *sanskars* through our own will power. Everyone has the same amount of will power. We need to realize and use it.
- The fifth set of *sanskars* are the original *sanskars* of every soul: purity, peace, love, bliss, knowledge, power and truth.

CHAPTER SEVEN

TAKE CHARGE OF YOUR THOUGHTS

SO: The mind plays hide-and-seek. The moment I try to see where it is, it vanishes. When I see my thoughts, they stop. When I focus elsewhere, they return. How do I control it?

SS: Let me share a story that I read. A disciple goes to his guru and asks for one word so that he can achieve what his guru has achieved. The guru says 'awareness'. The disciple writes down the word on a piece of paper and leaves. Halfway back, he wonders 'But what am I supposed to do?' So he goes back and asks his guru, 'What does the word mean?' Guru says 'awareness means awareness'. The disciple says okay and leaves again. Yet again he comes back and asks, 'But what does it mean and what am I supposed to do?' The guru says, 'awareness means awareness means awareness.' It means, do not try to find a logic behind it. Awareness means just be aware of your thoughts, just watch them. We are aware of everything happening in the world—under the ocean, on the moon, on other planets, in the neighbour's house—we are aware of what is happening everywhere. So, awareness means to know what's happening.

SO: Within me?
SS: Nothing within. That again is very complicated. When you say look within, where? Look at what? What are we supposed to do? Look within means just look at the thoughts that I create. Take a walk early in the morning. Don't just focus on who else is walking, what they are wearing, what they are listening, what they are discussing, or what is in the newspaper. Just talk to yourself—'What am I thinking?' You can practise this the whole day.

SO: People will feel I am talking to myself.
SS: You won't come to know when I am talking to myself. Just stop and check—What am I thinking?

SO: The moment I check what I am thinking, that thought stops. Some other thought takes over.
SS: This is because I haven't done it in a very long time. Once I do it regularly, I won't need to stop and look at what I am thinking. I will always be aware of what I am thinking. Suppose today has not been pleasant at work. I come home and sit with the newspaper. The television is on but my mind is not interested in it. I am thinking—'This shouldn't have happened; this is not the way they should have spoken to me. I have

been working so hard, but I just don't get recognised for my work.' Who is thinking all this? I am thinking. That's all. This is awareness. This is what I am thinking. The second stage of awareness is—is this the right kind of thinking for me? And third stage of awareness is: Can I change it?

SO: Do I ever stop thinking?
SS: There is never a stage when we are not thinking.

SO: The mind is always on. Does one have to consciously switch it over to something else?
SS: It's like water, flowing constantly. I can't stop it but I can always channelize it. I don't have to flow this side, I can flow the other side. So, I just change the direction of the water, give it a new direction to flow. Similarly, I don't stop thinking. A lot of people think meditation means to stop thinking, and so they will concentrate on a point of light and say 'no thoughts—no thoughts—no thoughts'. But 'I don't have to think' is also a thought.

The mind can never stop thinking. Let's not try doing what is not natural. That's why we feel very heavy in the mind. There is too much of pressure because we try to suppress something. It's not natural.

SO: The pressure to stop thinking leaves us tired and disappointed.
SS: Exactly. I cannot stop thinking, and then I say I tried meditation but couldn't do it. This happens with many people. There is so much going on in the mind; it is like a car that

is in the fifth gear and I suddenly want to bring it down to neutral. I am trying to do it in one go. What's going to happen? I get a jerk.

SO: I start being aware. What happens next?
SS: Practically, the first thing that happens is knowledge.

SO: Now I am aware that I am speaking to you. This is my thought and my question. What next?
SS: First thing is to be aware is that I am creating this thought. A very common illusion is that the thought comes to me because of a stimulus. A lot of people use this language: 'that thought just came to me.' What does it mean?

SO: 'He reminded me of that. He made me think. He made me do...' The language is wrong.
SS: Yes. The expression is wrong because the belief systems are incorrect. 'I was just hit by those feelings, by those thoughts.' As though something comes from outside. Thoughts don't come to us and feelings don't come from outside. However tough the situation may be, I am the creator of my thoughts. The minute I understand I am the creator, blame game is over.

SO: I am aware of my thought. I am the creator of this thought. Then I will analyse whether it is a bad thought, it will hurt me or disturb me. Am I right?
SS: Absolutely. I will be able to change the thought once I take responsibility that I am the creator.

SO: Responsibility is hard work. I may say I am ready to take responsibility but I never really understand it.

SS: Because the attention is always outside. We were aware of what is happening outside. Then we felt things happening inside. But because we were focused on the outside, we were not aware that what was happening inside was our creation, and that we had a choice.

SO: You had shared once that a child trips against a table while playing and falls. Parents console that child blaming the table; they tell the child 'The table is bad'. The child also feels better; he doesn't understand it was his mistake. So the conditioning for blame begins in childhood, that the table is in the wrong place.

SS: This is true. The child should be made to understand that the table was where it is supposed to be; it is the child who failed to see the table while playing.

Suppose my boss was rude to me. I had worked very hard, I was sincere and I finished everything on time. Yet he was unhappy. So my mind starts a commentary, 'He doesn't respect sincerity; he doesn't appreciate efforts.' I feel these thoughts are just coming to me. But who is responsible for them? I say it's my boss, and that I am justified in thinking this way. And next I say my boss needs to change. This is the moment we lose self-awareness and self-responsibility.

SO: If I am aware, then I will know that I am creating this thought towards my boss and that I am also sending negative energy to him.

SS: Not just that, the energy that I am creating and sending to him is also affecting me and those around me. My family with whom I spend the evening can feel that energy too, because I am creating it. It's like a perfume. Like it or not, I do get the fragrance of the perfume you have used. That's why if we are under stress, we automatically pass it on to our children.

SO: I have noticed that whenever I come home stressed or angry, even my dog just goes to a corner instead of greeting me.
SS: Now we will need to change the way we think. We create about 40,000 to 50,000 thoughts in a day. This translates into 25 to 30 thoughts per minute, created without awareness. One can imagine the quality of life we are living when we say 'thoughts just come'. It is like, you are the chairman of a company that has 40,000 to 50,000 products coming out of the factory on a daily basis. Yet you are not even aware of the product quality. Chaos becomes obvious.

Broadly, we can classify thoughts into four types: Pure, powerful, positive thoughts are the first category. They will be absolutely clean and selfless. These attributes are rare today. Selfless means thinking more about the needs and happiness of other people than your own, with no expectations attached. Wherever there will be an expectation it will be followed by hurt, so it's not positive anymore. Second category is of negative thoughts, which have resentment, hatred, criticism, anger, and these come in large numbers. Third category is of necessary or neutral thoughts but are of what we need to do—'I have to do this. I have to go here. I have to meet so and so.' We need to ensure necessary thoughts should not be followed by negative thoughts. Suppose the necessary thought is 'I have to go to the airport.' It should not be followed up with—'I hope there is no traffic jam on the way. I hope I will reach in time.' The fourth category of thoughts is waste thoughts, thoughts about whatever is not in our control. Thinking about what is not in our control is a waste of time and energy—in this case I think either about the past or about the future. Both are not in my control.

SO: Past, future, and even thinking about other people is wasteful.
SS: Even when I am thinking about other people—'They should have done this. Why did they do this? I want them to do this'—it's either in the past or in the future. I don't accept them in the present moment as they are. If we just practise this for one day, if we are just aware for one day, we will be surprised to see what we think about.

We think either about something that has already happened or about something still to happen. So we are living either in the past or in the future. Both are a waste because both are not in our control.

SO: I was once driving home from work, thinking of the movie scene I had just rehearsed. As the scene kept playing in my mind, I crossed my home. I had to then take a U-turn and go back.
SS: We can cross our whole life if we are like this, thinking about the past or the future. Just be constantly aware—first is the knowledge that I am the creator of the thought. Second is the awareness of the different types of thoughts.

Negative and waste thoughts are damaging. Waste thoughts are a waste of energy and they in turn are followed by several more negative thoughts. The minute I go into the past, the thoughts run along these lines—'It should have been like this; it should not have been like that. Those days were better. They shouldn't have said this.' If I go into the future, my thoughts can be—'When this happens then I will be happy...what if that happens...' This means now I am not happy, so these are not right thoughts.

SO: That's why people say 'I didn't do much today, yet I am tired'.
SS: Yes, if the mind was occupied meaningfully, it wouldn't have been creating so many negative and waste thoughts. It would have concentrated on something else. 40,000 to 50,000 thoughts a day is a lot. If they are not of the right quality, what happens to the system inside? Psychiatrists estimate that on an average, 80% of the time, our mind is in the past and 15% of the time it is in the future. So 95% of our thoughts go for a waste.

SO: Of the 80% thoughts about our past, I wonder how much is positive.
SS: There is nothing positive in the past, because if it was a pleasant past and I am thinking about it, chances are that I feel those days were better. So there is nothing positive there. People say it is good to have nice memories. Yes, it's a memory, but it's past. It's over. What is important is 'now'.

SO: People often speak about their past, about their jobs, the respect they had, and so on.

SS: What we feel within at such times is 'Those were the good times, but today I don't have that kind of attention.' So, by churning on the past, we may try to seek attention from people.

We speak very few words in comparison to how much we think. There could be 25 to 30 thoughts per minute but not 25 to 30 sentences. One may not speak even 4 to 5 sentences a minute. Every thought has an effect on every cell of the body. Thoughts are the most powerful source of energy that we have. Let's use them carefully. It's like nuclear energy—you can use it to heal or to destroy the world—the energy is the same. MRI, CT scans are done with nuclear energy on one hand, and nuclear missiles are available on the other. They are the same energy. Every form of energy can be used for constructive as well as destructive purpose. It's the same with thought energy. It can give and create love, peace, purity. It can also give and create hatred, resentment, worry, anxiety. It's the same thought energy. The wonderful part is that these are my thoughts, so I have a choice.

SO: Every thought has an effect on my body. With thousands of thoughts per day, what will happen to my body?
SS: Doctors today say most of our illnesses are psychosomatic—due to the mind-body connection. If we heal the mind, the body will start healing. Of course, we must take care of the body, but it will not be of much use if we take care only of the body without healing the mind. We meet people who are vegetarian, having clean habits, focussed on fitness, and yet have a heart attack at the age of 30 or 40. That's because they took care only of the body, while the mind was stressed.

Relax and reflect on these thoughts. Meditate.

Let me sit back, relax, and look at my mind. No one else will come to know that I am looking. It's something that goes on inside. And I am going to do it the whole day, while I am working, while I am talking, while I am driving, while I am walking; it's about just being aware of my thoughts.

My thoughts, my creation... something that I thought was happening automatically... I now realise the seed is me... I am the creator of every thought... every thought has an influence on my body... and on everyone around me.... Let me look at my thoughts... flowing beautifully... in control... because I realize I am the master.... Whatever happens around me... pleasant or not so nice... whatever anyone may do or say... however anyone may behave... I just sit back and look at my thoughts... and gradually channelise the thoughts into a different direction... because I am the master and the creator.... I turn the focus from outside to inside... because I understand now that the energy flows from inside me to everyone outside... So I am doing everything outside but my attention is on what I am creating inside... because what I create inside naturally flows outside.... I am honest with myself... honest in my thoughts... words and actions... and there is absolute harmony. This is trust.... I trust myself... I love myself... because I am a pure being.... Om Shanti!

MANTRAS FOR HAPPINESS UNLIMITED

- Self-awareness means to watch my thoughts, to be able to see what I am thinking and to be aware that I am the creator of these thoughts.
- The next step of awareness is to check whether these thoughts are of the right quality and healthy for me.
- We create 25 to 30 thoughts per minute, so 40,000 to 50,000 thoughts in a day. Thoughts are the most powerful source of energy we have. Let's be careful how we use them.
- There are four types of thoughts. *Pure* thoughts: powerful, positive and selfless; *Negative* thoughts of ego and anger that create hatred, resentment, fear, rejection, or criticism.
- Third category is of *necessary* thoughts, which are related to actions; these are neutral, yet they can be pre cursors to negative thoughts.
- The fourth category is of *waste* thoughts, which are thoughts about the past or the future—both not in our control, and so a waste of time and energy.

CHAPTER EIGHT

THE ART OF SCRIPTING
YOUR LIFE'S STORY

SO: After we spoke about awareness, I started speaking softly (I usually speak loudly) and my hand movements were not jerky. Everything felt peaceful, light and stable.

SS: It proves that when you take care of the mind, everything else is taken care of. It is the mind that has an effect on the body, which creates words and they finally come into action. When we talk about transformation, we say—'I want to change this habit. I want to change this part of my personality. I want to change this particular behaviour'—we always try to bring about transformation outside. The way I walk, the way I talk, the way I speak, the way I behave... we tell others also to behave in particular ways. Such a transformation is temporary because the seed is the 'thought'. Not changing the thought will have a temporary effect. We go back to the old self soon. However, if I change the thought,

I may not even be aware but I will find huge transformation outside.

SO: So we won't need to work on each aspect of our body—our movement, speech, body language. Method acting teaches actors to go from within to the outside. If I start believing I am so and so, I perform that role to perfection, naturally.
SS: I am creating the character inside. The whole sketch is there inside. Who does this inner work? My mind.

SO: Once you believe, things just happen. You are not acting anymore. You are living, you are playing.
SS: You are naturally flowing. Similarly, I am a peaceful being. I have created the character inside, so now I don't have to take care of how to speak, how to walk, how to behave. Once I am convinced inside that I—the actor—am a peaceful being, then everything that the actor will do will be through the vibration of peace.

SO: I should play the role of a peaceful personality. Suresh Oberoi as a peaceful being, happy being.
SS: You need to come back to the root first—I, the peaceful being, who has this name, this body and plays this role. Whether it's an actor, a doctor, a lawyer, it doesn't matter what the role is.

SO: So the peaceful being doesn't have to learn each and every step since he is peaceful.
SS: Each one of us is an actor and playing so many roles. In

your career as a movie actor, let's say you played 300 roles, but every role had that stamp of you as the actor—only you played it in that way. If another actor copies you and plays the same roles, he will be different from you because he has his own style. So the actor's personality will always reflect in every role he plays.

So now I have to remember, who am I the actor and what are the roles I play? So whichever role I play—a father, a husband, a friend, a boss—the actor's personality has to show in every role. Now who am I the actor? I am a pure, peaceful, love-full being. And it doesn't matter whether I am talking to a friend or to my son, the peaceful personality will reflect in both. The reason I am different with different people today is that here I am a friend, and there I am a father.

SO: I have to play a father here, so I will order my child.
SS: I have become more conscious of the role, rather than the actor who is playing the role. Old belief systems show that a father should behave a certain way. So I am behaving according to those set patterns of how a father should be— maybe authoritative, controlling or strict.

SO: If I am different with one person, speak differently to another, there is no consistency.
SS: Because I have been role-conscious. I am a friend of this person, so I speak cheerfully. There I am the boss, so I behave with my juniors in a certain way. The actor inside is just not aware.

SO: But everybody does that—different at office, at home, with wife, with friends, and so on.

SS: Which one of these is our original nature?

SO: I don't know. There are so many roles.

SS: Let's take a simple example. We walk into an office and within 10 minutes we meet four people: one from the security, one at the reception, then someone in middle management, and finally the CEO. Four people in 10 minutes, and our behaviour changes four times. My way of talking to the security guard and my way of talking to the CEO are different. Out of these four, which one is my original personality?

SO: I am confused. I am playing different roles so I don't have a consistent role.

SS: My original personality is missing because I am changing every time. I talked to a security guard, I talked to a receptionist, and accordingly I changed. Next I talked to a manager and so I changed; then I talked to the CEO, and I changed again. I connected to positions, to status, to physical looks, to all the things that are acquired.

SO: But people say what is wrong in it? Everybody does it.

SS: We don't know if it's normal, but yes, we have been doing it for a very long time. We are talking and connecting to people on the basis of everything that's acquired. Today you are the chairman, tomorrow you are not, so tomorrow my relationship with you will change. This means there was no relationship with you at all. And that's why relationships are so fragile. I can change my behaviour towards you, the minute anything that you have acquired has changed.

We are forgetting who we are. This acquired self is the ego. It is acquired by knowledge, by position, by wealth, by property. Everything that I have acquired—they are not me, they just belong to me. But when I am in the consciousness of 'This is what I have acquired' and 'This is what you have acquired', it is the 'acquired entities' talking to each other, not the people. And that's why there isn't a strong foundation. It's the ego of one talking to the ego of the other. When egos are talking, it is a position talking to a position, a bank balance talking to another bank balance. What about the pure being talking to another pure being?

This is where we really need to stop and realize that we are always connecting only to the outside, while the actor is dormant inside. Even if I find that actors around me are in slumber and I awaken, others will gradually wake up. When you are doing theatre, what do you do when one actor forgets his lines?

SO: I use his line, give him a cue, try to help out, or improvise it so that the act goes on.
SS: To be able to do that, what do you concentrate on? Suppose I am the actor and I forget my script. For you to help me, you will have to first pay attention to your script, right? You have two options. One, you pay attention to your script and just flow in the right way so that I will get the cue and I will also start flowing in the right direction. Two, you also get affected by the fact that I have forgotten my

script, because of which your attention deviates from your script. You are more interested in telling me how and what I should be speaking.

We are mostly focussed on other people's script today... what they should be doing, what they should be saying, how they should be behaving. In the process, we are not aware of our own script, what I should be thinking, what I should be saying. Throughout the day, how many times are we writing other people's script? We actually sit in front of the television writing the script for a minister, for a cricketer, for an actor—'They shouldn't be acting like this. They shouldn't be wearing this. This is not how they should have done this'. We waste time and energy by writing their script. Let's write only our script, because that is the only one that will be followed.

I can keep on writing your script—how you should be, how you should talk, how you should perform, how you should behave. Will you follow my script? No. What a waste of time and energy. I write the scripts of so many co-actors in my life, and none of them are going to use my script.

SO: It is so futile to be doing that and wasting time.
SS: At a time, you can write only one script. If I am writing yours, I am definitely not writing mine. Look at it this way—suppose you start saying something loudly to me, which I do not like.

Now, instead of taking care of how I should respond, I start telling you, 'This is not how you should be talking to me'. While I am trying to change your script, I go out of control. Soon I forget my own script and I start speaking louder and ruder than you did. When I start to write your script and forget my own lines, what happens to the play?

SO: Becomes a disaster.
SS: We see that happening everywhere today. If we just focus on our script, everyone else will take their cue. Someone next to you is getting angry, has lost his temper, is going out of control. But if you remain in control, he will soon come back into control because you have retained your composure. You are writing your script and they will come back to their original quality of peace. The other possibility is that, soon both of you will forget your script and go out of control. This is a choice we need to make—of writing our own script, because that's the only worthwhile thing to do. Our other thoughts about them are wasteful. This is awareness. I am aware of how many times in the day I just keep thinking about what other people should be doing and saying.

SO: But why can't I just stop myself and ask what is the point, why am I wasting time?
SS: Now that we are aware, we will do. Earlier we were not aware, we thought it was natural to think that way. If you see a tap running, you immediately close it because water is getting wasted.

SO: Our energy also depletes unnecessarily.
SS: It depletes because we are thinking of what is not in our control.

SO: Every thought has an effect on our body.
SS: The health of our body reflects the quality of our thoughts.

SO: Earlier I believed anger is natural. Once, someone who owed me money cheated me. It was so painful, I used to beat him up in my thoughts. I ended up having high blood pressure.
SS: In this situation, someone has cheated you of money. There's no denying that it is a grave situation. But let us keep our loss only till there. I have lost money and that was not in my control. Somebody else was responsible for it. But if I lose my peace of mind, physical health, harmony in my relationships, I am responsible.

I can say I lost the money because of him. But for anything else that I lose, I am the reason. This is what I do to myself.

SO: I was being irresponsible but I had thought it was natural.
SS: Let's remember one thing: What I think I am doing to others, I am actually doing it to myself. If I am giving a cold shoulder to someone or speaking angrily, it is actually a cold shoulder to me and anger towards me. This is because, whatever I create is first getting created in my mind. This means I am the first one to experience it. The cold shoulder that I give you might not affect you at all, but since I created the thought, I am bound to get affected. When doing something for other people, good or bad, it's less for them and more for ourselves.

SO: A healthy thought, a healthy body, a healthy life.
SS: We need to nurture pure thoughts, loving thoughts,

forgiving thoughts. Somebody has done something wrong, but I just forgive and forget. I am actually not forgiving him—I am forgiving myself. If I hold on to resentment and hatred, it's not for the other person, it stays in me, in my mind. I create it and I am going experience it. So, the entire responsibility comes back to me.

SO: I met a Brahma Kumar who told me somebody cheated him of 50,000 rupees. But he created a thought, 'May God give him so much that he does not repeat this act with anybody else. He must be in deep need. May God give him ten times more money, so no one else is cheated like I have been'. After eight years, the man who cheated returned with the money.

SS: Your acquaintance sent him good vibrations, good wishes—pure energy. So the person returned him the money after eight years. The question is—What was the quality of the mind for those eight years? Your acquaintance created this thought that maybe the other person who took the money needed it badly and was needy. He even blessed the person to have much more. In other words, he was at peace. The other option for him was to harbour hatred, resentment and revenge. He would still get back the money after eight years, but he would have done so much damage to himself by then, that the money would not be able to repair it.

SO: Let's do a small meditation.
SS: Relax and reflect on these thoughts. Meditate.

Let me look at myself... I, my own friend, honest with myself.... Let me look at the various reactions I give to other people during the day... anger... jealousy... criticism... hatred... seemed to be normal in return for what they have done to me. But now I need to stop and ask myself... who am I giving it to. It's a creation that I experience first... it's an energy that I am feeding to my own mind. Let me stop and ask myself... who is the one who is hurting me... who is the one who is creating the pain... I have a choice... I the pure and peaceful being... the actor playing so many different roles with other actors... each one playing their role.... I the actor remember my true personality... the pure being... I play every act and every role with the awareness of my original personality.... Look at yourself... that pure being as the parent... the friend... the boss.... Everywhere I go... it's me... the pure being. Om Shanti!

MANTRAS FOR HAPPINESS UNLIMITED

- If we change our thoughts, our words and actions too will change. Hence, personality transformation begins with our thoughts.
- When we interact with people, let us interact with the soul, the pure being, rather than the acquired body, positions and achievements. When we talk through the consciousness of our acquired labels, then it is the ego of one talking to the ego of the other.
- In any situation, we are playing our role along with so many actors. Let us stop writing their script because they are not in our control. Let us write only our script. When we keep thinking of what others are doing, we are only depleting our energy.

CHAPTER NINE

YOUR DESTINY: FATE OR FREE WILL?

SO: Thoughts occur too quickly to be aware or control them. Once I am getting angry, I'm able to stop in some time. But I want that awareness before anger triggers.

SS: This frankly is great start, to be at least aware. You are able to stop there right in the middle. It means if earlier you were going to stay angry for 10 minutes, now you will probably finish in a minute.

SO: Something within reminds me to take control.

SS: Because we have changed our definition of what is natural. Earlier we said anger was natural, so we gave ourselves the liberty to get angry. We believed anger was needed to get work done.

By justifying anger, we did not find the need to change.

Now we are experimenting with a new belief system that peace is natural and we want peace. We understand it is our own *sanskar*. So when you get angry, you realize you are going against your natural self and stop.

SO: Wouldn't people consider us weak if we quietly listen to unpleasant things without reacting?
SS: What is more important: how I feel or what people feel? This is a critical question. We need to check carefully; answer may be different for each of us. For some, their own personal well-being is more important and for some, other people's opinion matters more.

SO: I will say both, but honestly mine is more important.
SS: Let's visualise two colleagues—one of them screams and hurls abuses at the other. So the other person reacts likewise and screams even louder. Would we call this strength? In the same situation, suppose the second person remains calm and stable, understanding that it is not the right time to explain his perspective. Not only does he remain composed outwardly, but he empathizes and retains his good wishes for him. If you are a spectator in this scene, would you call this weakness?

Let's not even evaluate if it is strength or weakness; let's just see which behaviour is better. If someone shouts at us, is it easier to shout back or to remain internally stable?

SO: Remaining stable is extremely difficult.
SS: Yes, so that's where strength comes in.

SO: Doing something difficult amounts to strength, is it?
SS: Yes, because it requires strength to do something difficult. If I have to lift this chair, it requires strength. If I say I can't, that is my physical weakness. To do something against the tide of negative energy, to remain protected first and then create positive energy against the tide of negative energy, requires a tremendous strength. To shout back and then justify that the other person shouted first doesn't require any strength at all.

SO: When we would get bullied at school, we got taunted if we remained quiet without reacting.
SS: When bullied, we were quiet outwardly but internally we were disturbed. If a boss shouts at me, I can't say anything back because of his position. But internally I am not stable and it starts having an impact on me. People may say I should have argued and finished the matter. They say it is better to get angry rather than suppress it. But here we are not talking about suppressing anger; we are talking about simply not creating that turbulent energy of anger at all. That is strength.

SO: People hear so much from their bosses, but internally they are in pain.
SS: So they are already creating anger. It's a silent form of anger and internal. Anger is anger, whether it is in the form of hurt, hatred or verbal abuse. It will affect you. But once I start taking care of my thoughts and feelings, I can first stop showing anger outside, and gradually stop creating it inside. Then it will not matter whether it's my boss or my child, the rule remains the same.

SO: How does one acquire this kind of mental stability?
SS: First, understand that anger is not strength. It's an absolute weakness because in those moments I have gone out of emotional control. And going out of control is not strength.

SO: If anger is not strength, what is anger? Is it frustration or an inferiority complex?
SS: Anger is the whole turbulence that takes place inside. I justify it and I blame the world for what I am feeling, and I want to retaliate. The anger could be because of one person and it might show up on another. We vent our anger in various ways and towards various people. I can't show my anger to my boss, so I shout at my wife when I come home. My wife may not hit back at me, so she vents out her anger at the child.

I can't say I didn't get angry at all. It's just that I accumulated it inside. I didn't vent it but then I created it, and eventually took it out on someone or the other. When we understand this mechanism, we will be paying attention. Every time I create a thought, what's the next thing that happens?

SO: After the thought will be the action.
SS: That's at a later stage. What happens just after I create the thought?

SO: When I create a thought, I am creating certain emotions.
SS: Yes. Immediately after I create a thought, a feeling is created. Sometimes we are not aware of our thoughts, but we are aware of our feelings. We say—'I am not feeling very nice today'. We are not sure what is the thought behind that feeling, but we

are aware that we are not feeling nice. Any feeling is a result of a thought we create. So, if we are not aware of thoughts, let us just be aware of how we feel. For example, 'I have to meet you'—this is a thought I create. Based on my past experiences or what I have heard about you, it will immediately generate a feeling. Thought is always followed by a feeling.

All my feelings put together, develop my attitude. A thought about you is followed by a feeling subsequently. And because this has happened several times, an attitude towards you is also created. We talk about 'changing our attitude', but it cannot directly change our attitude. We need to change our thoughts, so that our attitude will automatically change.

SO: How to change the thought?
SS: Sit back, check, choose and change.

SO: With awareness and practice. And awareness itself is practice.
SS: Gradually you will find that your attitude has changed.

SO: Then it becomes automatic.
SS: It is in the process plant.

SO: The basis is awareness of your thoughts, isn't it?
SS: There is a stage even prior to that. We will see that later. Now let's consider the subsequent stages—thought, feeling, attitude, and action. If I have a positive attitude towards you, my way of talking and behaving with you will be a certain way. If I have a negative attitude, everything will be different.

SO: I am reminded of my movie director calling out 'action' and I start enacting my scene. He says 'cut' and I stop.
SS: We can do this throughout the day—action and then cut. In your profession you have a retake, but we don't have it in life. When shooting for a movie, despite the retakes you pay attention each time. In life, where there is no retake, we hardly pay attention. Every thought that I create has an impact on me and my body and the people around me. Suppose for 10 minutes I create thoughts of pain, and in the 11th minute I say 'Enough now' and stop. But now I cannot change those 10 minutes of pain. That's why constant awareness is a must. It comes with practice. Gradually 10 minutes will reduce to 8...5...3, and then we will be able to say 'It's okay, this is it.' Finally we reach a stage where we will not be creating pain. We will be aware of it as soon as we are about to create it and say 'Okay, change.'

SO: So one day we won't create it at all.
SS: Yes, because then I have come into the consciousness of my original self—that of a pure being. We are right now in the transition stage. It's like we are sleeping and trying to wake up. We wake up and say 'Let me sleep for 5 more minutes.' Right now we wake up to the truth that we are peaceful beings but then we create anger once more, and that is we fall asleep again.

SO: One has to believe first. If I tell somebody he is a peaceful being, he will ask for proof. Is it because everyone yearns for peace?
SS: We only yearn for what we are. The body is made of five

elements of nature: water, air, ether, fire and earth. Whenever there is lack of even one of them, we immediately seek it. We say 'I want water,' or 'I want fresh air.' Why do I need them? Because our body is made of them and lacking them right now. At those moments if you offer me anything else, I will reject.

Similarly, I the being am made up of seven elements: purity, peace, power, love, knowledge, truth and bliss. Every time there is an imbalance, we say: I want peace, I want happiness, I want love, or I want power.

The method may be different but everyone is looking for the same things. I can be using anger as a tool, but I am never comfortable when I am angry. Anger is not my nature; it is an acquired 'sanskar,' an acquired personality trait.

SO: Probably that is why we like to be in the company of a saint, or go to a place of worship.
SS: Yes, because we come closer to our natural self. We feel nice watching sunrise and sunsets. But stuck in the middle of a traffic jam we don't feel nice. Why? Chaos is not our natural self. A place or person or a situation that makes us feel closer to what we actually are, makes us feel nice as well.

SO: So the 7 elements or qualities are me. How does one have them all the time?
SS: We need to understand the complete process. First I am changing my thought from 'I want peace' to 'I am peace.' When my thought changes, my feeling will change, my attitude will change, and my action will change. Now my actions will not be focussed on seeking peace, because now I know that I am

peace. My actions will arise out of my nature of peace.

Any action repeated a number of times becomes a habit. All my habits put together create my personality. So who I am today, or my personality today, is a package of every thought I create. Personality development programmes teach us to talk this way, smile that way and so on, but these outer gestures will not help if we are unhappy within. How can I smile if I am not happy? Even if I smile, what energy do I radiate? So, personality begins in the mind.

So the inner mechanism is this: thought—feeling—attitude—action—habit—personality. Now, we come to the last and most important step—This personality goes out into the world, working, socializing and being with family, so at every step I am creating my destiny.

It starts with thoughts and leads up to destiny.

SO: So every thought is creating destiny? And life is a manifestation of one's thoughts?
SS: We are willing to do anything to change our destiny today. We go to an astrologer, to a numerologist, to a tarot card reader. We want them to predict our destiny, and if it's not what we like, then we ask them to do something to change our destiny. The truth is that no one else can change our destiny.

SO: How can we change our thinking?
SS: The first step is to realize its importance. Earlier we would say 'They did this to me, so I had to react'. But now we are aware that what we think creates our destiny. We were confused about destiny. We said 'It was my fate, my luck'. But who

decided the fate? Since we didn't know who it was, we said God decided it. We put the blame on someone else because we were not ready to take responsibility. The fact is, I am creating my destiny. The energy that I send out is my 'karma' and the same energy, when it comes back in the form of situations or people, is my 'destiny'. An astrologer might ask us to wear a ring to improve our life's situation. We obey and wear that ring. When we wear the ring, we create a thought, 'Now things will be better for me'. So things become fine because we use the ring as a stimulus to change our thoughts, and thereby change our destiny.

SO: Does it boil down to having faith in that ring?
SS: Yes. If I wear the ring without faith, it will not work.

SO: Someone can write a particular prayer, put it into a *taweez*. We wear it around the neck believing that no black magic or evil eye will thereafter affect us. We become sure that nothing wrong can happen. So our thoughts change.
SS: For how long are you able to create that thought after wearing it? If we are not aware, this thought will be there for a few days. After that, the ring or *taweez* is just a part of the body.

SO: I never thought of this. I feel if I wear it, my negativities finish and I will be happy. I forget it after sometime and go back to my old nature. I haven't changed myself at the core.
SS: You used the ring as a stimulant to change your thought. Until you are aware of the ring, you are creating the right

thought and the belief that 'Now everything will be okay, no one can harm me'. This was the thought that you required—either with or without the ring. But because you are wearing the ring, faith in the ring makes it easier to create these thoughts. One month down the line the ring is just a part of your body and you lose the awareness of wearing it. Chances are that again you will go back to the old thought process—'They did this to me; they did that to me.' When you forget that you are wearing the ring, then the effect will not be there.

SO: Is the stimulus creating my thought?
SS: Stimulus does not create my thought. I use the stimulus to create my thought.

SO: I am creating my thought because of the stimulus. Can we do the same without the ring?
SS: You are creating the thought, not the ring.

SO: Can we have a meditation?
SS: Relax and reflect on these thoughts. Meditate.

My life... my journey.... I am writing the script... as I create every thought.... I am writing my own destiny... let me be aware that no situation is happening on its own... I have written my destiny.... Whatever is happening to me now... I had written the script for it much earlier.... What I am doing now... what I think now... I am writing my script for my present and for my future.... The control... the power is totally with me.... Let me be awake and aware that I am the scriptwriter of my destiny... I the powerful being.... I am not influenced by situations and people... focus and attention on my thoughts manifesting into my destiny. Om Shanti!

MANTRAS FOR HAPPINESS UNLIMITED

- If other people are behaving in a reactive manner, my remaining internally stable, is strength. So peace is strength, not a weakness.
- Anger is not strength. It is a sign that I have lost control of myself. Even hurt, resentment, are silent forms of anger that damage me, the creator.
- My every THOUGHT is followed by a FEELING. If I am not feeling nice, I have to stop and check what I have been thinking.
- My feelings over a period of time develop my ATTITUDE about people, situations, work or about the world.
- My attitude comes into ACTION. Any action done repeatedly becomes my HABIT. All my habits put together create my PERSONALITY. At every step, this PERSONALITY determines my DESTINY.
- I, the being, am an embodiment of 7 qualities—Purity, Peace, Love, Bliss, Knowledge, Power and Truth.

CHAPTER TEN

FEELING GOOD FROM
THE INSIDE-OUT

SO: We discussed about life being a manifestation of one's thoughts. We also discussed about the essence of future predictions.

SS: We need to understand it in the right perspective. Astrology, numerology, or any other similar branch that predicts our future is a science. People who have studied those science over a period have mastered it. They are like doctors who have studied the body thoroughly. Suppose I consult a doctor with my blood-test reports, he may say there is a probability that in the future I am at risk of getting diabetes. He makes that assessment based on my genetic factors, my current lifestyle and on present health parameters. Going back home with the new information and I have two ways of responding. One—I start thinking, 'I will have diabetes, it is sure to happen because my mother has it, my grandmother has it, I have so much stress, my lifestyle is very erratic, even the doctor has predicted. I am going to have diabetes.' The doctor said that I 'may' get it within a year, if don't take the right measures. But with my negative attitude, it is possible that I will get it within six months. The stress that I create with the doctor's information will precipitate the disease. And ultimately, I will say the doctor was right.

The other option I have after I receive this information from the doctor is to take complete charge of myself. I bring about a shift in my lifestyle. I start walking daily, I do meditation, pranayam and yoga. I change my food habits and sleep timings. I take care of my emotions and lead a healthy lifestyle. There is a big chance that I will never have diabetes. The doctor's assessment will not come true in this case.

It is all about how we respond to an assessment or prediction. There was a probability of my getting diabetes, so that part was pure science. But it was still a probability, not a reality. I considered that probability as a warning signal and changed my lifestyle. The assessment became invalid because I took charge. But if I don't take charge and I just accept the probability as an upcoming reality, it is going to become the reality. I have accepted it already, I have created anxiety and worry, and so it is going to happen because the probability was already there.

In the same way, I go to an astrologer. He might say based on the planets, the moon, the stars, their positions right now, that there is a probability that something unpleasant will happen in the next six months—a probability of physical health getting affected or business facing obstacles, or someone trying to harm you. It's only a probability, not yet a reality. This is very important to understand that it's a probability predicted by someone who understands the science. So, we thank them for making this prediction and giving us the probability, but now we need to take charge.

SO: Should we take it as a warning and do something to ensure that the prediction doesn't manifest?
SS: Yes, but only if we have the power to listen to the information and not get influenced by it. What happens, unfortunately, is that when somebody gives us a prediction, we accept it as a reality. We say 'This IS going to happen, because an expert has said this, and his predictions for so many people have come true. It's going to come true in my case as well.' By creating this thought, we have already converted the probability into a reality. Our mind accepts that it is going to happen. Thoughts create destiny, and so it happens.

SO: Perhaps that expert's predictions had come true in the past, so we tend to believe him.
SS: True. It is pure science and there is nothing wrong about predictions. It's a probability, but people may accept the prediction as a reality. The mind accepts it, so it manifests as reality.

SO: But don't predictions help to change destiny?
SS: There are two ways. Suppose someone predicts that my next 6 months are going to be challenging since planetary movements are not favourable. They say whatever I do, I am

not going to be successful. It's a prediction. If I don't know this prediction, I don't know this piece of information. So I put in all my efforts. Obstacles do come, but I overcome them because I am motivated to succeed. I want success and I am working for success. I don't get demotivated by obstacles.

The other option is I know the prediction that success is difficult because of unfavourable planetary movements. This information can be so dominant in my mind that I may not be able to raise my thoughts over it. I start my business but I my thoughts are—'What is the use when I know I cannot be successful in these 6 months? Whatever I do, there is going to be a problem.' Now, even when I am faced with the smallest of obstacles, I reiterate that this was bound to happen. So I lose the enthusiasm needed to overcome the obstacle.

SO: So, it is safer not to have this piece of information.
SS: Either you don't seek predictions, or you develop the ability to elevate your thoughts higher than the prediction. Take it as a challenge.

SO: My thoughts should be, 'I am peace; I am bliss; I am knowledge; I am powerful.'
SS: Absolutely. Now where is the obstacle? The obstacle can only be outside. The only thing required to face it is stability inside.

SO: Even a child falls so many times before he learns how to walk.
SS: Each time he falls, he gets up and starts walking again.

Suppose somebody predicts—'You are not going to get up for the next 6 months, try as much as you want. You are only going to fall.' If I accept this prediction, the very first time I fall, I might say, 'Forget it, I will try after 6 months. There is no point trying until then.' So I don't even try with the right energy, and because I don't create the right thoughts, I don't get the right destiny.

On hearing the prediction, we ask them for a solution to be successful in these 6 months. Then we are asked to wear a particular colour, a particular finger ring and so on. Do the planets change positions when we do that? No, they are still the same. But we are doing something that is helping us to change our thoughts. First, we had the information that these 6 months would not go right for us, and so we were demotivated. Now we have the information that if we wear this particular finger ring, success is certain. We create the thought, 'I am wearing this and now I am going to cross any obstacle. My success is certain.'

SO: It is said that the rays of the Sun pass through the stone and enter our skin.
SS: I, the being, is energy. I have vibrations. As will be the qualities of the being—love, peace, purity—so will be the aura of the person. The photographs of deities always feature a white light around the head, which symbolizes purity of the soul. If the soul is pure, the aura is white. If there are toxic emotions, the aura could be towards red, blue, or grey. By using an external stimulus, we try to change the colour of our aura, which then will have an effect on the mind. So, we are going

from outside to inside. But the easiest way will be to change my thought, so that my aura will automatically change, my vibrations will change, my situations will change.

SO: Basically the colours and stones are changing our aura?
SS: Yes, they do work, but the extent and duration need to be evaluated. Someone asks you to wear a red shirt for things to be better. How often can one wear a red colour shirt? Why not just create powerful thoughts instead? We believe that the easiest method is to change something outside, to experience a change inside. It's actually about changing something inside, to experience results outside. The process is inside-out, not outside-in. The inside is in my control and I have the power to make a permanent change.

SO: When you do it from outside, you do not have complete control. Moreover, predictions do go wrong at times.
SS: They were not predicting reality; they were predicting a probability. We need to remember this. We have no right to say anything to them. A probability always comes with a certain percentage attached. They may predict that your next 6 months will be beautiful, but if you are demotivated inside, nothing will be smooth. So the prediction turns out to be wrong.

We have been discussing about the effect of external influences on our mind. We saw how our mind can go beyond the influence of situations, objects and people. If my mind can do that, then we can also go beyond the influence of planets. Planets are also an external influence. They do have an influence, but we choose whether to get overpowered by it, or rise above their influence. When we are weak internally, everything will have a bigger influence on us—someone's smallest word will disturb us because we are weak. The mind will not have the power to cope, accommodate and pack up unwanted thoughts. So your one word can upset me for days or even for 6 months. If your one word can upset me for the next 6 months, the planets' movement can also upset me for the next 6 months. It is all about rising above external influences.

SO: Basically I choose whether to get disturbed or not.
SS: Yes. Sometimes they say, 'You don't get along well with your spouse because you bedroom is in so-and-so direction. Change your bedroom, and the change in direction will bring harmony.'

Is it necessary that everyone whose house is in the right direction has a good relationship? No. If this had to work, then everyone would just change the direction of their house, wear particular stones, and live blissfully. Many of us are following what they say, but pain and failure still there.

SO: But it has worked for people.
SS: For some time, yes. They create a thought, 'I have done this, now my relationship will be good.' Six months down the line, they would have forgotten that they changed the direction of their room. North, south, east, west—these are energies, magnetic fields. Each direction is a field and it will have its effect. But the highest field is here (in the mind). If we are determined to get along with each other no matter what, then we actually create harmony regardless of the room's direction.

On the other hand, if we cannot get along, then we end up with conflicts even in the best-designed house. It's about the mind being ready to take the challenge. We cannot keep changing everything outside. I can change the house, but can I change the other person? I can only change the way I think.

SO: But they share examples of how change in direction brings energy.
SS: Absolutely. It is science so there is no doubt about that. But there is a science, an energy that is more powerful than the energy of alphabets, numbers or planets. It is my own energy, the energy of the consciousness.

SO: I am weak internally if I rely on other energies. I have a much stronger energy within me.
SS: If I can't take charge of my mind, I try to take charge of everything else outside. When should I begin a new business, what direction should my office face, which stone should I wear, what symbol should be displayed in my office... I take care of everything around me, because I don't have the power to take care of my thoughts.

SO: I have a bigger power within yet I seek peace from weaker powers.
SS: The weaker we become, the more we look outside. The lesser control I have on myself, the more my power is reducing, because I am not taking care. If you don't discipline your child at the right time, he will lose his way eventually.

SO: What care is to be taken?
SS: Discipline the mind, be aware, take care, and choose the right thought.

SO: It is very important to understand who I am, how powerful I am. If I am peace, I don't 'want' it anymore.
SS: Yes, I don't have to 'do' anything to be peaceful.

SO: I don't say 'please give me some power.' I am power. Why will I need it?
SS: We will not need at least externally. Everything external is needed for physical comfort—for fun, excitement or entertainment. But not for peace and happiness.

SO: I used to get disappointed that I took my family for a holiday to make them happy, but my child came back unhappy.
SS: Be happy and then go for the holiday. Don't go for a holiday to be happy.

I am not going on the holiday for happiness. I am going for fun, for a change of routine. That's all that a holiday is. So holiday will not be for pursuing happiness, it will be for expressing and sharing the happiness that we are already filled with. Our perspective changes from taking to giving, so we look forward to meeting people, we look forward to being with everybody, so that we can radiate our happiness to them. Not so that they can make us happy.

I am a peaceful and happy, but I get to experience it and express it only when I am in interaction with someone. If I am sitting by myself, I don't get to express or experience my own qualities, and that's why relationships are so important. Unless I come into interactions, unless I have an exchange of energy, I will not be expressing and experiencing. I experience my quality only when it comes out. When I give anger to you, I first experience it. Similarly, when I give peace to you, I first experience it. I experience my happiness only when I am in interaction with someone, so I look forward to going to work, I look forward to meeting family and friends—not for wanting but for expressing and experiencing, and therefore sharing.

SO: It feels so nice when our good qualities radiate naturally and we are not trying hard.
SS: We are 'human beings', but today we have become 'human doings.' We are doing so many things. Let us 'be' what we are supposed to be. Spirituality says 'Be happy and do this, because you are a human being, doing an action.'

SO: Human being, doing an action. Let's have a meditation.
SS: Relax and reflect on these thoughts.

> *This body is my costume... it is just a machine.... I am the controller and the operator of this machine.... Consciousness... energy... the spiritual being... my original sanskar is purity, peace and happiness.... Let me look at myself...consciousness at the centre of the forehead... the operator sitting there taking charge of this machine... playing roles... relationships and responsibilities.... I the human being doing action... but*

as I do... I express what I am.... Let me look at myself driving to work... at office with my colleagues... at home with my friends and family... with the awareness... I am a pure being doing things... interacting with people.... and thereby expressing and experiencing my original sanskar of peace and happiness.... Let me see how the day will be. Om Shanti!

MANTRAS FOR HAPPINESS UNLIMITED

- People predicting our future are only telling us a probability. It is only a probability, not a reality.
- We have the power to listen to the prediction and still choose our response—our thoughts and actions—and thereby create a reality based on our choice.
- We believe we need to do things outside to change the way we feel inside. The reality is we need to change how we feel inside, to change things outside.
- Happiness cannot be obtained from other people. It is to be created within and shared with the people we meet.
- We are not 'human doings' who do different things to be at peace. We are 'human beings'. We need to be at peace and then doing everything that needs to be done.

CHAPTER ELEVEN

ARE YOU EMOTIONALLY OVERWEIGHT?

SO: I was reading, 'What comes first: peace or happiness? Can you be at peace if you are not happy? Do you get happiness from external factors or from within? The mind is fickle like a fast galloping horse and the only way to control it is by involving it in good actions beneficial for all.' I need your help to understand this.

SS: The quotation says—'When you are at peace, you will be happy, depending on what your idea of happiness is. Whether you get it from outside or from inside.' Let us stop and check what outer happiness is. It's actually not outer happiness—it's an outer stimulus that I use to create happiness for myself.

SO: 'I create happiness'. Emphasis is on our creation. You never say, 'it gives me happiness.'

SS: At every step, when you are happy, when you are hurt,

or when you are upset, just stop and ask who is creating it. I am creating it, irrespective of the situation or stimulus. The more we are aware, the more we will understand that we have held people or situations responsible. Whereas, all the time it was we who were creating it. That is the awakening. Now we only need to take care of how to change what I am creating.

Without this understanding, we would feel powerless, because we believe people are responsible for our happiness and people are responsible for hurting us. We wait for them to be nice. At the same time, we hope they will always be nice to us. What if tomorrow they are rude? We will not be happy. There is dependency, and hence fear. When we understand that everything is happening in the mind, there is no insecurity or fear of the future. Situations could be pleasant or not so pleasant, people could be pleasant or not so pleasant. I only have to take care of one person—me. It becomes very simple.

You mentioned about the mind being fickle, and the only way to control it is by engaging in good acts that are beneficial for all. An indecisive and inconsistent mind is said to be fickle. When the mind keeps changing, the quality of thoughts is not very nice. When we are peaceful, our mind works slowly and cautiously. When we are worried, thoughts are very fast. When we are stable, the speed is slow. When we are fearful, the thoughts gain speed. So if my mind is fast and inconsistent, it means the quality of energy is not right. And now we want this mind to do an act that is for the good of others. Benevolence is not in the act, it is first in the energy that I send out while doing the act. Here again, by asking you to do a benevolent act that will control the mind, which is running haywire, we are putting the stress on 'doing something outside that will help you to be peaceful'.

SO: When I am in a bad mood, suppose I listen to music or start dancing, it changes my mood. The mind is not as agitated as before. So the outside-in approach works to an extent.

SS: Outside-in approach works only to an extent and only sometimes. People say we need to count to 10 when angry. But often, we don't even realize before we react out of anger. If we had that awareness—that now I am angry, that I need to stop and drink water, or that I count numbers—we would be aware enough not to react.

SO: So we come back to just being aware.

SS: Yes. These are only minor suggestions for us to pause, take a break, and work on our mind. Like you said, dancing takes my mind to a calmer position, to understand. So you have just given your mind a little gap. If I am upset about something, instead of confronting you right now, I take a little gap. Now what is that little gap for? Just to ensure I don't confront you right now. I postpone my external reaction. The internal reaction is there. But I resolve the issue internally and then decide how to respond. There is a difference between reaction and response. Reaction is automated and not in my control. Response means I think, understand and then act. That's why we try and bring in those time gaps. But quite often, reaction is so fast that the time gap is lost.

SO: When I was running a business, I would write many letters in anger in the night, after closing down office. I would keep the letters to post the next morning, but I never posted them.

SS: When the mind works very fast, it is wise to postpone our reaction till it slows down. Then we see the situation in a different perspective and then choose to respond differently. This is what we are trying to achieve. We are also trying to keep the mind working at the right, steady speed always.

SO: We again go back to awareness.

SS: Yes. If you are aware, the speed is fine. Suppose a young child is playing in the room. If the parent is not looking at the child, he will do whatever he wants. He may fiddle, drop or break things. Now if the parent just stands in a corner and starts watching the child—not saying or doing anything, but just watching the child, he becomes aware and withdraws from mischievous activities.

SO: So we need to watch this inner child that is our mind.

SS: That's the journey, and it is not going to happen in one day. Have you been able to do it sometimes?

SO: Yes.

SS: That's the proof that we can do it.

SO: But I feel my mind doesn't like this kind of monitoring.

SS: A child never likes to be disciplined, because he is used to running around and doing what he wants. Suddenly if I tell the child I am going to take charge of him and that he has to obey me, he may not like it. But gradually the mind gets used to this way of thinking because it is going to be at ease. Even the mind is tired now, as it has been working at a very fast pace.

SO: Can we switch it off like we switch off the engine of a car.
SS: We cannot switch off the mind even when we are fast asleep at night, forget switching off in the day. We need to understand why the mind works like this and the influencing factors. We know about positive thinking, yet negative and waste thinking comes naturally. What are the factors that influence the quality of thoughts? In any situation, the thought I create is influenced by three factors.

One factor is past experiences. If I had an interaction with you before, if I had done business with you before, I have a past experience. Every time I think of you, my quality of thoughts will be based on those past experiences. If it had been a pleasant experience, my mind creates nice thoughts. Second factor is information. Everything that I take in through my sense organs—what I read, what I watch, what I eat—everything that is going in has an effect on the mind. Information plays a vital role on the mind. The mind is very clean soon after waking in the morning after being well rested. So it is fresh and ready to create, and ready to absorb. In the morning we usually read the newspaper or switch on news channels. This means we are reading, listening and watching about terror, violence, natural calamities, financial issues, social and political upheaval, and so on. The mind, which is like a clean blotting paper, absorbs this chaotic information. The kind of information will influence the thoughts. Information is the food, thoughts are the resultant energy. If I have eaten the right food, I am going to be healthy. If I have not been eating the right food for the mind, my emotional immunity is going to suffer.

SO: Whatever we are taking in through media, through surroundings, affect the quality of our thoughts, is it?
SS: Negative information will certainly give rise to negative thoughts. Because that's the raw food that I have taken in. Thoughts are creating my destiny as per the inner mechanism, but what's creating the thoughts is the raw food, which is information. So, if I want to take charge of my thoughts, if I want to change the quality of my thoughts, I will have to first change the quality of the raw material that goes in. During the first two hours of the morning, the absorption power of the mind is very high. If we are reading, watching and listening to negative content during this time, though we want positive thinking, from where and how is it going to happen?

Moreover, suppose a child doesn't return home on time in the evening, and his phone is not reachable. It becomes so natural for parents to think that the child is in trouble. We need to assess why we feel that something could wrong have happened. Why are we creating a negative thought?

SO: And what is the kind of energy we are sending into the universe?
SS: Yes, suppose the parents wait for 30 minutes and we still can't get in touch with the child. What is going to be the quality

of thoughts as they wait, or in any other similar situation? But they will say—'Is it not natural to think negative? How can we believe everything is okay?'

SO: We fail to think that the child must have met a friend or gone to a movie, and unable to connect to the parents for some reason.
SS: How often are we able to think that someone is late because something nice must have happened? Negative thinking comes easily because that's the quality of information we have inside us. Even if we start with this simple practice of not watching the news or reading newspapers early in the morning, it brings about a big change. Protect yourself by not consuming toxic food in the morning. Just this simple practice will bring visible results.

SO: Then we will not blame situations; we will be responsible.
SS: Situation is a trigger and information is present inside. When a trigger comes, the quality of the thoughts created will be influenced by the quality of the information we have.

SO: When the child comes home, parents vent their worry and anger on him.
SS: That happens because for one hour they were creating only negative thoughts. This stimulant has just returned and parents think he is responsible for all that they created. So there it goes. All the toxic energy they created in that one hour of wait radiated as vibrations to the child and also to everyone around them. And then they say it was natural. No, this is not natural.

Natural is, the child has not returned on time and they are unable to contact him. The situation is not in their control. Let us always see immediately what is in my control and what is not. If the situation is in our control, take charge. Otherwise there is only one thing in our control—our quality of my thinking.

SO: But why is it easier to create a negative thought rather than positive?
SS: We just have to fill in a different quality of information. It's as simple as that. When I change the quality of the information coming in, my thoughts change, the way I respond changes, and my destiny changes. I have a choice. When the newspaper comes in the morning, I have a choice as to what time I will read it. So let's take this one resolve today and experience a big change. Postpone the newspaper and the television news to the later part of the day, and substitute it with very pure and powerful information. This simple change to our morning diet for the mind will make all the difference. So one positive step in the morning, and similar positive step just before going to sleep is the remedy. Today what are we taking in just before going to sleep? Television serials or horror movies. That's the last layer of information going in. The first layer of information in the morning influences our thoughts during the day. The last information before we go to sleep influences the quality of our thoughts at night.

Let's devote 10 minutes to reading something pure and powerful after we have finished our duties for the day. We have to fill in the information first because if we just sit and try to create positive thoughts, we won't be able to do it.

We need to change the last layer of information. Once we finish reading, we will sit back and reflect on that, unpack what has happened in the day. That's very important. Let's not sleep with unresolved issues. Situations had come up and there were times when we did not respond the right way. Reflecting on the day does not mean recalling everything that happened. Just reflect on the way we responded and see how else we could have responded.

SO: Can we have a meditation to follow before going to sleep?
SS: Relax and Reflect on these thoughts.

Let's sit back, with the body relaxed.... Just before going to sleep... let me look at the day.... An entire movie has passed scene after scene... with lots of actors around me acting according to their scripts.... Let me not get entangled in the situation.... Let me just watch myself playing the role... as a detached observer.... I will just focus on my performance... let me not look at the other actors in the scene... no judgement or comment.... I am looking at myself... my response and my script in every scene.... As a detached observer let me ask myself... was there any scene that I could have performed differently...? Did I have another choice to the way I was writing my script ...? Let me play the scene again on the screen of my mind... same scene but a different me... with a different script.... I am programming my mind and preparing my mind to a more powerful and a positive response for the next day.... Om Shanti!

MANTRAS FOR HAPPINESS UNLIMITED

- People ask us to count 1 to 10 when angry. These are external measures to postpone our reactions. However, if we take care of our thoughts, we will not even create thoughts of anger in the first place.
- Our thoughts are created based on our past experiences and the information that we take in through sense organs.
- During the first few hours in the morning, the absorption power of the mind is at its highest. We need to take care of the quality of information we take in then. To protect ourselves from creating negative thoughts, we need to avoid newspapers, news channels or anything that has disturbing information, early in the morning.
- Try a new way of living, to be able to create pure, powerful, positive thoughts naturally. Let us begin the day with reading or listening to pure and positive information.
- The last layer of information at night influences the quality of thoughts while sleeping. So let's end the day with 15 minutes of reading or listening to pure and pleasant information, and resolve any issues on the mind.

CHAPTER TWELVE

GET COMFORTABLE WITH YOUR MIND

SO: How important is our belief system, for happiness?
SS: We have seen the entire internal mechanism—where every thought I create gives rise to a feeling, and the feeling develops my attitude. The attitude comes out as action, repeated action becomes habit. Habit develops my personality and my personality determines my destiny. This is the process from thought to destiny. So every thought becomes very important. But what determines the quality of my thought? Everyone is talking about positive thinking, yet why does negative thinking come so naturally the minute there is a stimulus or a trigger? The factors that determine the quality of our thoughts are past experiences and the information we consume. These two play a very important role in the quality of our thoughts.

The third and the most important factor is our belief system. Our body is like a computer: I the soul is the operator, and the belief system is our operating system. As will be the operating system, so will be the way the software will run on the machine. Certain software run on a particular operating system, while others run on an operating system. The computer is important, its operator is important, but the operating system plays a huge role. At times a virus can attack the computer's operating system and hampers functioning. This is comparable to a certain wrong belief, which can hamper the way we think, and alter our destiny. Spirituality will help us install an antivirus. Many people use a computer but do not install antivirus in the machine, so time and again the system tends to get corrupt.

SO: They also don't see its expiry date.
SS: Yes, you need to update your operating system. What is the sign that my system crashes once in a while? Outbursts of anger, pain, or being hurt are signs of a system crash. It's time to understand and check how often my system crashes in the whole day.

SO: So many people are irritable throughout the day.
SS: And then they call it natural and their natural behaviour. They say, 'This is how I am.'

SO: They also insist that somebody else has passed the virus on to them.
SS: Even if someone passes a virus to me, it's still my responsibility to counter it with an antivirus. No one else is going to give me the antivirus. Times are getting tougher,

situations are challenging, people are increasingly vulnerable. Suppose I have known you for years, but your temperament and behaviour has suddenly changed. I have known you to behave in a particular way, so I don't expect you to behave differently. Let's say your nature is to be jovial and carefree, but you are going through a conflict so your temperament has changed. I am used to you talking to me humorously. So now I can't understand why you have withdrawn and not interacting the same way.

SO: What is your role and my role in this case?
SS: My first responsibility will be to take care of myself and not get hurt. Otherwise, that is where friendships and relationships suffer. If I get hurt, then I am only nursing my own wounds. If I am hurt because you did not talk to me properly, I cannot help you. I take it personally and start feeling you are angry with me. I assume you do not respect me anymore. While I am creating all this pain, I do not understand that your changed behaviour is not because of me, but because you are in pain for some reason. Since I am in pain, I will not be able to help you to heal.

SO: But why does other people's behaviour matter so much to us?
SS: Since we seek acceptance, appreciation and approval from people around us. The magnitude will vary, but acceptance and approval from people around us seem to have become a foundation for our self-esteem.

SO: Why do we often misunderstand people?
SS: We misunderstand because we are hurt. We are in pain. When in pain we will never see the situation in the right perspective.

SO: That is when it's easier to misunderstand than understand.
SS: Your shirt is white in colour. But if I wear different-coloured glasses or lens, it will appear a different colour to me. You are who you are, but if I wear a different colour or perspective every time because of my pain, my hurt or my ego, then you will appear different to me. This creates misunderstanding.
We need to clean our own lenses or windows. We shouldn't ask them to change what they are wearing.

SO: Do meditation in the morning and night help us clean our perspective?
SS: Absolutely. If there is emotional blockage or a negative thought I will look at everyone through that window. If I have been hurt because of something that happened with you and I am in pain, I carry that pain with me to everyone I meet. So I will see everyone through that pain. If I have been rejected by you and my self-esteem is low, then my self-esteem will be low with everyone. It doesn't happen that my self-esteem is low only when I am with you and is high when I am with someone else.

SO: But some people do make us feel comfortable. They raise our self-esteem.
SS: But we cannot be dependent on people to lower or raise

our self-esteem. If I find 5 people who help me raise my self-esteem, I may meet 50 who can bring it down.

SO: That is why people find their own comfort zone of family or friends.
SS: But who provides this comfort zone? Even within family and friends, there are many who will lower our self-esteem.

SO: Out of 20 family members, we are comfortable with just 4 or 5. But our topic itself is 'happiness unlimited', and by choosing such comfort zones, we are limiting ourselves.
SS: Let us say being with you raises my self-esteem, because you accept me unconditionally. But you are able to do that only when you are in a stable state of mind. Tomorrow, if you go through some problem, you lose your capacity to accept me unconditionally.

SO: Not only when I am in a problem. But tomorrow I may just not like what you do and my behaviour towards you can change.
SS: Absolutely. I was comfortable in your company till today, but now I have to prove myself to you. And as soon as I start to prove myself, there will be fear. I am not sure if you are happy with me, whether I have been able to prove myself right. In this process I am not sending the right energy.

SO: We come back to the point that one has to be independent.
SS: 'In-dependent': dependent only on that one who is inside.

Let's not be 'out-dependent' because things outside will change and they have a reason for changing.

SO: Does that make us a little recluse?
SS: Let's always remember that in order to heal and to help others, I will have to be healed first. If I am healed, I will be there for other people. If I am in pain, I can never be there for anyone else. I have to first take care of myself to be there for others selflessly.

SO: Does this amount to selfishness, but in a positive manner?
SS: This is the foundation for being selfless. Today even when we are doing something for others, it is less with the intention of giving and more with the intention of taking. Even while doing for others, we are satisfying some vacuum within ourselves. So it is actually being selfish.

SO: That makes self-care necessary, to take care of others.
SS: The equation flows this way: Only a healthy person will be able to heal others, will be able to understand others. Without understanding my thinking, my attitude, I cannot understand why you are feeling a certain way. I am not ready to understand why I am hurt, but I want to understand why you are upset. How is it going to happen?

The wonderful part is, when we understand how our mechanism works, understanding others becomes easy. If I am hurt, I will immediately be able to realize that I am hurt. I understand the reason and check my attitude. It's up to me how long I want to remain like that. Now if I see someone who is upset, I can go beyond the visible hurt to see what they must be going through, for them to behave that way. It becomes easier to be with people. We don't look only at their criticism, we look at the dynamics inside that person's mind, for them to be so critical. So, we just have to understand our mechanism—then we can understand everyone else's.

SO: One of my neighbours was always angry and ready to pick up fights. When I complained about him to another neighbour, she said, 'Poor chap, he must be in some kind of pain to behave like that.' Now I understand what she meant. Understanding others is very difficult. If my wife's behaviour changes, I never ask her if something is wrong. I just get irritated and leave her alone to manage it herself. Why couldn't I ask her if she needed any help?

SS: This is withdrawal. When we can't handle other people's temperaments, we withdraw. Even if it is temporary, even if it is for one hour, when the other person is in pain, we withdraw. Think of your wife getting angry or behaving in a slightly different manner. It could be a sign that she needs help. However, you move one step behind and think you will come back later. But right now she needs you more. It's because you are not able to take care of yourself that you move away. This is not support. We are not there for each other emotionally, though physically we are living in the same house. We are not there to heal each other because we have not healed ourselves.

Suppose you are sitting with a friend, and your son walks into the room. He doesn't greet you but just walks past both of you. The thoughts that come to the mind are, 'What's wrong with him? Where are his manners? My friend would think I haven't brought up my son the right way. He may tell others about my son; what will everyone else think about me?' So here we are nursing our own wounds. My responsibility is to not to question why the child is behaving like this, but to see what is the pain within him that caused him to behave that way. Now if you go to his room and question his behaviour, your child will request you to leave him alone. When the parent has been hurt or felt disrespected, the child will not want to be with the parent at that moment. Right now the child is in pain, and he doesn't want to be with anyone else who is in pain.

You will love to meet somebody who is absolutely stable and is accepting you unconditionally, extending unconditional support. We don't get this from too many people today. Unconditional acceptance means I do not fluctuate internally, irrespective of your temperament. And I am not judgmental about you. The energy we receive from someone who accepts us unconditionally heals our pain.

SO: Don't we fluctuate automatically? If you raise your voice, I raise my voice. If you are soft, I am soft. If you smile, I also smile.
SS: We keep changing our behaviour according to everyone else. Because of this, we tend to forget our original qualities. My sari is white in colour but if I meet somebody in red, I paint it red. When I meet somebody in black, I paint it black, and when I meet somebody in green, I paint it green. At the end of the day there is no white left. So where is my personality? I coloured my personality according to everyone

else's personality. And it's actually not their personality either; it's my perspective about their personality. We don't know people as they actually are.

SO: Are we not capable of knowing?
SS: We won't be capable when we are seeing them through our perspective. There is only one person who knows me well and that's my own self. No one else can claim that they know me very well. No, they know me through their perspective and that perspective keeps changing.

SO: So a child knows his father from his own perspective.
SS: Absolutely. The same father will get along with his three children in different ways, because the children see him in different perspectives. One might be very scared but that's because he or she is weak. Second child could be very confident and comfortable running to him. The third child might just stand in the corner, neither scared nor comfortable. The father's nature and personality are the same. So if one is comfortable, why is another scared? One has a meek personality, so he sees the same father through his perspective.

SO: If we consider the example of a couple: If a husband is tough, the wife says 'Can't you speak softly?' In some other situation she may say 'Can't you be tough sometimes?' So we are not happy with one kind of role our partner plays. We want them to be different at different times.
SS: Because that wife has mentally created an image of a right husband. We get into a relationship with the image of an ideal partner or an ideal friend. Then we spend our lifetime trying to

change the person to fit into that image. Let's say my image is that of a partner who is an extrovert, dynamic and loud. But if I have a partner who is soft, quiet, and an introvert, I will not like his nature. So it's not about how he is as an individual; it's about what image I created of him in my mind. I will keep on saying, 'This is not how you should be, you should be loud, you should be more open, you should be like this, you should be like that...' And even if he becomes an extrovert, I might say, 'You should not be so outgoing...' Basically I will want the person to be exactly the way I imagine him to be. It's like going to a tailor who will stitch your costume according to the measurement that he prefers. He tells you that you have to change your body to fit into what he stitches. He doesn't create the costume according to your measurement.

And that's why we keep fluctuating. We keep changing according to what everybody wants.

SO: We fluctuate because of them or because we are not stable?
SS: What happens if I meet 10 people, and I feel my happiness is dependent on making these 10 people happy? Each of them expects to be a different kind of person. If I keep changing, where is my original self? I will eventually get suffocated because I am struggling to change.

SO: How do I come out of this struggle? Also, can we have a meditation?
SS: Actually in our innate system, there is a core that never gets corrupt. That's the consciousness. Meditation is the process

of passing those layers of belief system and reaching that core, which is the spiritual energy.

Relax and reflect on these thoughts. Meditate.

Different people I meet the entire day have different personalities... each one is operating through their belief systems... their rights... their wrongs... their perspectives.... Let me look at myself... through which perspective do I interact with each individual I meet.... Is it an influence of their personality... am I changing according to everyone I meet... or am I able to hold on to my internal, pure, original personality... Let me look at myself today the entire day... meeting about twenty people.... Let me see myself with each one of them... interacting through the core of my personality... my original sanskar of purity and cleanliness.... I the flawless, perfect, pure being... uninfluenced and undisturbed... by anything and anyone around me. Om Shanti!

MANTRAS FOR HAPPINESS UNLIMITED

- There is only one person who knows me well—that is my own self.
- Our thoughts are created based on past experiences, information we take in, and our belief systems.
- Its important to take charge of how we feel, instead of being dependent on others. To be IN-DEPENDENT means to be dependent only on the one inside. Don't rely on things outside because they keep changing and they always have reasons for changing.
- Let us be ourselves and not keep changing our behaviour according to how others behave with us.

CHAPTER THIRTEEN

CHOOSE HAPPINESS, NO MATTER WHAT

SO: Sister Shivani, how much do past experiences influence our mind?

SS: We cannot avoid our past experiences. They are already recorded in our memory, but we can try not to play the same record repeatedly. Because every time we play it, we are converting the past into the present. We are creating the same emotions all over again, and every time we create the same emotion, we deepen the *sanskar*. When it comes to recalling bitter past experiences, it is like deepening a wound by scratching it. It's a past wound; we need to heal it. But if we open the Band-Aid from time to time and scratch it, how will the wound get healed? Sometimes we also get others to join us to discuss a painful event. So our wound never heals. The past has passed. Full stop. No comma, no question mark, no exclamation mark. No why, what, how... just a full stop, so that we are able to move ahead, fresh and clean, and now what we create will get recorded. People say we remember the past because we have to learn from the past, but what do we have to learn from there? We just have to check the way we responded in that scene, and learn if there was a more comfortable or better way to have responded. Other than that, there is nothing to learn from a past situation. We only have to learn from our response. Holding on to things, not letting them go, accumulating emotions and reliving them will only cause more pain. It's like you are holding something in your hand for hours: the weight of the object remains the same but the hand will start hurting after a while.

SO: People complain of chronic headaches, skin diseases, and even doctors sometimes cannot diagnose the reason.
SS: Because we are holding on to the past. We need to remember that it's over. It's the past, not in our control.

SO: But if something tragic happened in my past and a friend asks me what the matter is, I will share with him.
SS: It is comparable to opening up the Band-Aid put on our physical wound, and scrubbing the wound. We had gone through so much in the past. But when we think about it again, we experience the same pain all over again. So we need to ask ourselves, 'How many times am I going to relive the same painful emotions?' More importantly, anything done repeatedly becomes my personality, and then I carry that personality with me everywhere. We may not discuss the past with everyone, but because it's in our mind, that pain becomes a part of our vibrations.

SO: Don't we also attract such people and such situations?
SS: We are not attracting situations, but we are responding to situations in a similar manner as before. If there is a challenge, since we are already emotionally low, we don't have the power to face the situation in a proactive way. I am already hurt about something that happened years back, and here comes another fresh stimulus. I don't have the strength. The pain that I will create will be much more than what I would have created, had I healed my past. Also, the pain created because of one particular situation or person, does not remain only in that relationship with that person. The pain has now become a part of my personality, and I will tend to get hurt more easily in other relationships too.

SO: So it becomes a vicious cycle of pain and more pain.
SS: Because it's my personality, not theirs. I can use you as the stimulus and say I am hurt, but now it's my personality. This personality will go with me to every situation and every person. So I am vulnerable every time. When there is a challenge, it's not about changing your job, it's not about changing your partner, your friends, your spouse. It's about making yourself stronger. And then your emotional immunity system is strong, no matter where you are and who you are with. You will get along with any person or situation.

SO: Is it easy to change thoughts?
SS: People are creating miracles in their lives. They themselves are doing it; no one else does it for them. The first realisation is—IT'S ME, NOT THEM. We are responsible for how we

feel; we have no one to blame. I have seen couples who were on the verge of divorce coming back to a happy married life, with only one understanding—it's not him or her, it's me who needs inner work. This is when things will change.

SO: In a divorce, it's usually a blame game.
SS: In a divorce it is usually about, 'You are wrong.' Now we understand, it's my response to the situation, irrespective of his or her behaviour. So, we start focusing on our response.

SO: They will say 'If you speak like this, then naturally I will respond like this'. How do you still change?
SS: So that is the realisation. 'You speak like this,' but now I will choose how I am going to respond. The equation has changed. I got a phone call from a 24-year-old married woman, standing on the terrace of her house and wanting to jump down. As a last resort, she just called up and said, 'I don't want to live and I was about to jump down, but I thought I will just call up and find out if you have a solution. My husband is having an affair with somebody in the office and he wants to divorce me. I see no reason to live.' She was totally shattered. 'What about my parents, society and others?' At that moment I was speechless. I said, 'Okay, first come down. So what is it that you want?' She said, 'I want everything to be back to normal like it was. I want my family life, my married life to be what it was.' I said, 'Create a thought that everything is fine'. She said, 'But everything is not fine'. I said, 'I know, but what do you want?' She replied, 'I want everything to be fine.' I said,

'Now create a thought that everything is fine and my husband is absolutely fine, nothing wrong has happened.'

For about 10 days, we spoke for almost an hour daily on the phone. She used to say, 'Everything is not fine. How can I create this thought that everything is fine? What should I do? Should I go and talk to that girl? Should I go and talk to that girl's parents? Should I go and talk to my husband's parents? What should I do?' I had to repeatedly get her back to creating the same thought, that everything was fine. Finally she started working on changing her thought. She started repeating, 'Everything is fine. My husband is absolutely fine. Nothing wrong has happened.' She stopped crying also, and she eventually became more stable. Now when her husband came back from work, she wouldn't be crying or weeping. This provoked him even more. He would be abusive and find faults with her, because he was trying to justify his own action. She had to remain stable and just keep telling herself, 'Everything is okay, I am in charge of the situation, and I am in charge of myself.'

After one month, her husband handed over the divorce paper to her, saying his company was sending him to the USA and that the other girl working in the office was also going. They were going to get married there. She called me up and told me what happened. Then she surprised me by saying, 'You know, I am fine. I think I will be able to take care of myself. I will take up a job and I will be able to live with my parents.' In one month she had changed her thoughts. The situation was the same as it was one month ago, but she had changed her thoughts. She just worked hard on herself. The husband left.

Two months later he called up from the USA and said he wanted to come back. She called me up and asked 'What should I do?' I asked, 'What do you want?' She said, 'I want everything to be back to normal.'

SO: That's what she always wanted.
SS: Yes. And today it's more than four years since that episode. They are living together happily and have a daughter too. All the effort was made by her. The knowledge that we learn at Brahma Kumaris and its simplicity makes it easy to adopt and implement. People have to just take up the challenge and make that effort initially.

SO: Did she feel a sense of failure when the husband was leaving to the US?
SS: It was not a failure. We were not looking at the situation; we were only concentrating on her being able to take charge of her mind. Situations are not in our control. We expect that spirituality or religion will change our problems. No, they won't. Problems and challenges will arise; obstacles are going to be there. Spirituality gives us the power to take charge of the self and then face the situation.

SO: But when she was creating the thoughts that everything is fine, she was trying to change the situation.
SS: She was changing her thoughts.

SO: Wasn't she changing the situation in her imagination?
SS: She was not imagining. Everything was fine in her

mind. It's always in the mind first. I have to be okay internally.

SO: But what kind of visualisation did you give her? You said 'Just think that everything is fine; nothing is wrong.'
SS: If a partner or a child is drifting away in a relationship, what's the energy that we send out to them? Anger or hurt. Someone is already drifting away and we are sending out negative energy. It will only take them further away. If you want the person to come back, you have to send powerful positive energy. For that, we need to stop being critical and judgmental about that person. We need to respect them as we always did, and so we need to create the thought that nothing wrong has happened. From the other person's perspective, they have logic for what they are doing. We may find it wrong but they have a reason.

I have spoken to so many families where there is a conflict between partners or between parent and children. If you talk to both parties, you will never be able to decide who is right and who is wrong, because none of them is wrong. You listen to one and you will say, 'Perfect, this person is absolutely right.' And when you listen to the other person, what they say will make equal sense as well. So it's just that each one is right from their own perspective. Now all that we have to do is, show them each other's perspective.

SO: We can approach the situation with understanding and knowledge.
SS: Let me share about another couple. The wife had been living

separately for the last three months because the husband used to abuse her. After 10 years of bearing the physical violence, she finally took her daughter and left. She met me to see if any solution was possible. She was constantly weeping while talking about it. I asked her how her husband's childhood had been. She said it was not pleasant. He was a single child to working parents. They did not spend enough time with him, so he had been very lonely. What I understood was that the husband felt he had not got love from others around him. In his wife, he found a person to call his own, and used abuse to show power and control over her. It was actually because he was insecure and possessive, and he was in a lot of pain inside. When I explained this to the wife, instead of hatred she was now filled with empathy. She said, 'My husband was in pain all this while, and I thought I was the one in pain.' This reality changed her, and now they are healing each other.

It's not that the situation is solved in one day, because the husband says he doesn't know why he gets so aggressive. Such things happen because of emotional blockages. It's just that we need to be able to detach ourselves from our point of view, see the other person's view, and understand what provoked their behaviour. But what had happened is when the husband mistreated her, the wife could feel only her own hurt. She could not understand what he was going through, and vice versa.

SO: What if both of them had a bad childhood?
SS: Both of them came to me next time. The wife was constantly weeping. She kept insisting on the husband 'Promise me that you will never hit me again, only then will I come home.' The

husband said 'I promise I will try.' She said, 'No, give me a guarantee that you will never do it again'. So I told the lady, 'You guarantee that you are never going to cry again.' She promptly said 'I will try.' It's so easy to tell other people to change, because we don't have control over our own *sanskar*.

SO: But can we change the *sanskars*?
SS: Absolutely. By understanding and seeing what the reason is.

SO: How can I find the reason within me? It takes 'you' to find it or can 'I' find it? Suppose I get angry very easily; how do I know what kind of *sanskars* I have? Will I have to go through my past?
SS: You definitely need to check your past. Suppose someone has had a troubled childhood—maybe parents were critical, physically abusive, or any other reason. The child always has to try to keep proving himself, and still keep going through pain because of the criticism received. Now, as this child grows up, he builds a defence mechanism. He does not want to continue going through the hurt and pain, and so he becomes loud and aggressive. Before anyone can say anything to him, he tends to snap at them. People will start fearing him. This is a protection wall that the person builds, so that no one will muster the guts to say anything to him. But on the inside, he is an innocent, fearful and hurt child.

SO: He had gone through some situations that he could not fight.
SS: Not only that, the child experienced hurt at that time.

Now the child doesn't want to get hurt again, and this will be so even when he is 30, 40 or 50 years old. Only when this person consciously starts working on himself and says, 'I will not get hurt even if someone says something,' he starts becoming strong inside.

Now he can drop this artificial defence mechanism and be his natural, polite, humble self with everyone.

SO: Does being aware of thoughts help us detach from our views?

SS: Absolutely, because when we detach from our own perspective, we see the larger picture. Like in the case of this couple, the wife could see only her perspective and say, 'How can my husband abuse me? He does not love me' he does not respect me.' What she is feeling is right, but she can see only her perspective. But when she detached from her perspective, she was able to see her husband's pain and his perspective. She then became stable. Her hatred turned into empathy.

We all talk about understanding people. We say we cannot understand the other person, which means we just cannot see their perspective, because we are so attached to ours.
Earlier we could see the situation only from our side, and from our side it was totally different. For me to be able to see from your side, I need to get up from this chair and then come and sit on that chair. For that, I have to detach myself from this chair. But if I am so stuck to my position, to my ideas of right, I won't even get up from here. When I get up to be on your side, that's empathy and understanding, and that strengthens relationships.

SO: You mentioned the other day, that when a person feels empty within, he tends to be angry. What does emptiness within mean?

SS: Vacuum. Many people will say they have everything in life, professionally, personally and materialistically. But inside there is something amiss. They are not even very sure what they are talking about.

SO: Is it some kind of an emotional fulfilment they are looking for?

SS: All that we were doing—studying, working, achieving, even building relationships—we were doing in order to get happiness and contentment. Today at the age of 30 or 40, we realise that we have got everything but we are still experiencing stress, anger and anxiety. So I am empty in the sense that I haven't got what I wanted, even though I got the whole list that I thought would give me contentment. So I say I am empty. While achieving external success, we might have even compromised a lot. That compromise made us empty. Peace is our nature, but we created anger. Honesty is our nature but we compromised on values at times. Humility is our nature but we created ego to feel powerful. Every time we were doing these things, we were going against our natural personality.

SO: But we feel bad about it, perhaps guilty too.

SS: Not only feel bad, we need to think of how the journey has been. Let's say this glass is full. Now I am on a journey towards my goal, but I have to take care that water in this glass should not spill. If I keep spilling the glass during the journey, some 10 years later I would have achieved everything but the glass will be empty by the time I reach there. Then I will say that I am empty because of the anger and resentment I created. I did everything possible to achieve what I wanted. It doesn't mean achievements are wrong. It's just that I should have taken care of this glass while moving towards my goals.

SO: But even before moving towards goals we were empty, weren't we?
SS: No, look at a child—always contented and serene. That's what is so attractive about the child. But later we condition the child's mind that in order to be happy, he has to get more marks. In order to come first, he has to be stressed and compete with friends.

SO: Can we have a meditation?
SS: Relax and reflect on these thoughts. Meditate.

> *Let us sit back and relax... preparing myself for a good sleep.... Let me just look at the day... everything that's passed is past... full stop.... However tough... however challenging... it's over.... Now is a new moment... a new response... and a new feeling.... I am in control.... I am pure energy.... I am already complete... beautiful... contented... successful.... Everything that I was looking for outside is already there in me.... The purpose of my life is not to achieve it outside... but to*

express it while I am moving through my goals... I am the complete... perfect... pure being... master of the body and every sense organ... everything in control. Om Shanti!

MANTRAS FOR HAPPINESS UNLIMITED

- Every time we think of the past, we are making it the present because we are recreating the same emotions.
- The past has passed. Full stop. Let it not repeat in the mind; when we do, it is like rubbing a wound and therefore not allowing it to heal.
- There is nothing to learn from the past, as the situation has already happened. The only thing we need to learn is whether we had the choice of responding in another manner.
- Holding on to the past—not letting go—will only create pain within. The situation is the same but the longer we hold on to it, the pain increases.
- In relationships, no one is ever wrong. Each one is right from their own perspective. Detaching from our perspective and understanding the other's perspective is empathy.
- While working towards our achievements, if we take care not to compromise on our values of peace, love and happiness, we will be always contented.

ABOUT BK SHIVANI

Spiritual Guide & Mentor,
Speaker & Writer

Since 1996, BK Shivani has been a practitioner and a teacher of Rajyoga Meditation, which is at the heart of the teachings of Brahma Kumaris World Spiritual Organization.

Intent on transforming human consciousness through spiritual education and emotional empowerment, she has been empowering millions across the world towards peace, health, happiness and harmony. She analyzes and addresses a broad spectrum of pertinent topics that include life skills, relationships, parenting, value education, leadership, emotional and mental wellness, work-life balance, overcoming addictions, the depths of spirituality, vibrational energies and frequencies, consciousness, meditation, karmic philosophy, religious beliefs, integration of science and spirituality and integration of mind, body and medicine, among others.

For her contribution in transforming millions of minds,

she was honoured in 2019 with the *Nari Shakti* award, the highest civilian award for women in India. For her enormous influence in empowering Spiritual Consciousness, she was conferred the Women of the Decade Achievers Award by ASSOCHAM'S Ladies League in 2014. Since 2017 she has been appointed as a Goodwill Ambassador by the World Psychiatric Association. During her multi-city tours to North America in 2017 and 2018, she was honored with Proclamations at Cupertino, New Jersey, Ohio, Santa Clara and San Francisco for reshaping lives.

At Silicon Valley, USA, she has addressed corporate giants such as Google, Microsoft, Cisco, Amazon and Intel. She has also spoken at business houses like Reliance Jio, Maruti Suzuki India, Indian Oil Corporation, Godrej Industries Ltd., GE Energy, Asian Paints, and Times Of India, to name a few. Apart from the YPO, FLO and EO Chapters, Indian Armed Forces, she also speaks at the Rotary International and Lions Clubs International. She has been invited by pan-Indian premier schools, colleges, management institutes and leadership institutes like IIM, IIT, AIMA and so on.

The Indian Medical Association of all the major cities of India have invited her for talks on mind-body-medicine. She also conducts programmes for cancer patients and cancer survivors. BK Shivani actively promotes Organ Donation initiatives every year. Besides, she is part of a team that along with FOGSI, has developed 'Adhbut Maatrutva', a unique programme that explores scientific and spiritual principles of Divine Garabh Sanskar, for expecting parents.

Besides being a gifted thinker, speaker and writer, BK

Shivani is a gold medallist for academic excellence in electronics engineering from the Pune University, India.

Readers can connect with her online on:
Facebook: https://www.facebook.com/BKShivani
YouTube: https://www.youtube.com/BKShivani
Instagram: https://www.instagram.com/BKShivani

THE BRAHMA KUMARIS

The Brahma Kumaris is an international NGO in general consultative status with the Economic and Social Council of the United Nations and in consultative status with UNICEF. With its global headquarters in Mt Abu, Rajasthan, through more than 4,500 centres in over 140 countries across 5 continents, the Brahma Kumaris offer a wide range of courses and programs to create positive change.

The Brahma Kumaris teaches Raj Yoga as a way of experiencing peace of mind and a positive approach to life. The organisation provides opportunities to people from all religious and cultural backgrounds to explore their own spirituality and learn skills of reflection and meditation derived from Raj Yoga, which will help develop inner calm, clear thinking and personal well-being. Since its inception, the organisation has made values like purity, peace, love and joy a practical and sustainable experience in the lives of millions of people worldwide.

At the heart of the organisation's teachings is the foundation course in Raja Yoga Meditation. This course provides a logical and practical understanding of the relationship between spirit and matter, as well as an understanding of the interplay between souls, God and the material world. All courses, seminar and workshops are offered to the public free of charge, as a community service.

The Foundation Course in Raj Yoga Meditation is offered free of charge at every centre of the Brahma Kumaris. It is a 7-day course, 1 hour daily. To know your nearest centre visit

https://www.brahmakumaris.com/centers/(India)
http://www.brahmakumaris.org/centre-locator
(International)

AWAKENING channel is a 24 hours TV channel of the Brahma Kumaris.

COURSES OFFERED BY BRAHMA KUMARIS

- Self-Management
- Stress-Free Living
- Living Values
- Emotional Intelligence
- Mind Management
- Harmony in Relationships
- Self-Empowerment
- Enhancing Self-Esteem
- Exploring Inner Powers
- Values in Health Care
- Leadership Skills
- Work-Life Balance
- Karmic Principles
- Art of Right Thinking
- Effective And Good Parenting
- Spiritual Advancement

In addition to the institution's centres, these courses are conducted at the place of work of the participants, including corporates, schools, hospitals, offices of private and public firms, and prisons.

AWAKENING
To A New Way of Living

Brahma Kumaris TV Channel

Awakening TV Channel by the Brahma Kumaris is created with the understanding that 'When We Change Our World Changes.' It showcases:

(1) Chat shows and Talk shows on Emotional health and Lifestyles issues such as Stress, Anger, Fear, Relationships, Professional Issues and Work-Life Balance.

(2) Programmes on the Mind-Body connection: Programmes on De-addiction, Reversal of Coronary Artery Disease, Diabetes, Yoga, Role of emotions in creating good health and healing a disease.

(3) Programmes on Mental Health Issues: Depression, OCD, Hyperactivity in Children and all mental health diseases prevalent in today's times.

(4) Programmes on the Application of Spiritual Principles in every Profession: Doctors, Jurists, Politicians, Administrators, Business & Industry, Media, Art & Culture, Scientist & Engineers, Security Services, Travel & Tourism and many more.

(5) Cookery shows presenting Sattvic recipes and sharing the role of mind during cooking and eating.

(6) Special programmes on Holistic Parenting.

(7) Guided meditations throughout the day to help people to meditate sitting at home.

(8) Devotional Songs

Website: https://awakeningtv.org

RAJYOGA MEDITATION COURSE

Self-Realisation – Recognising the self as a spiritual being, an infinitesimally tiny star, point of light – a soul. The intrinsic nature of the soul is that of love, peace, happiness, truth, bliss, purity.

Knowing God – Like us, God is also a soul, the Supreme Soul – who never takes a body of His own. He is the Almighty Authority, the Ocean of Love, Peace, Power and Purity.

Relationship with God – When you learn to tune your mind in meditation to the mind of God, then whatever the situation, you always have a source of help and strength to draw upon – an infinite reservoir of power and virtues that is only a thought away.

Law of Karma –Every action has an equal and opposite reaction. This means whatever we are presently experiencing is the return of what we once sent out. Our every thought, word and action is the energy we create and radiate - this is our KARMA. Situations and people's behaviour is the energy we receive - this is our DESTINY.

Raj Yoga Meditation - It is a meditation that can be practised anywhere at any time, with open eyes. Regular practice helps us to respond to situations, rather than just reacting to them. We begin to live with harmony, we create better and happier, healthier relationships and change our lives in a most positive way.

8 Spiritual Powers–We discover how to cope with every challenge and how to live well in every situation using the 8 powers of Raja Yoga: the power to withdraw, the power to pack up, the power to accommodate, the power to discriminate, the power of judgment, the power to face, the power to co-operate and the power to tolerate.

BRAHMA KUMARIS CENTRES

The Brahma Kumaris have more than 8,500 centres in over 133 countries, with the international headquarters at Mt. Abu, Rajasthan.

INDIA

World Headquarters 'Pandav Bhawan,'
Post Box No.2, Mt. Abu–307501
Tel: 2974–238261 To 238268

Om Shanti Retreat Centre
Gurgaon. Tel: 0124–2379960

Shanti Sarovar Retreat Centre
Hyderabad. Tel: 040–23005983

25, New Rohtak Road, Karol Bagh New Delhi.
Tel: 011–23628976

23, Dar-Ul-Muluk, Gamdevi Mumbai.
Tel: 022–23803681

81/1, Bangur Avenue, V.I.P. Road Side Kolkata.
Tel: 033–25747863

3702, Annanagar, Block Q–96 Chennai.
Tel: 044–26267441

UNITED KINGDOM & EUROPE

Global Co-operation House, 65–69 Pound Lane
London. Tel: 44–20–8727 3350

Global Retreat Centre
Oxford. Tel: 44–1865–343 551

Centre de Raja Yoga, 74 rue Orfila Paris, France.
Tel: 33–1–43 58 44 27

Raja Yoga Institut
Frankfurt, Germany. Tel: 49–69–49 18 46

Styrmansgatan 3 Stockholm, Sweden.
Tel: 46–8–663–79 59

12 rue J.-A. Gautier Geneva, Switzerland.
Tel: 41–22–731 12 35

RUSSIA

2 Gospitalnaya Ploschad
Moscow. Tel: 7–499–263 02 47

4 Severny Prospect
Saint-Petersburg. Tel: 7–812–293 28 44

NORTH & SOUTH AMERICA

Global Harmony House, 46 S. Middle Neck Road
New York. Tel: 1–516–773 0971

Peace Village— Learning & Retreat Centre
New York. Tel:1–518–589 5000

2428 Griffith Park Boulevard
Los Angeles. Tel: 1–323–664 0022

1212 New York Avenue
Washington DC. Tel: 202–238 3263

897 College Street Toronto, Canada.
Tel: 1–416–537 3034

Rua Dona Germaine Burchard, 589
Sau Paulo, Brazil. Tel: 55–11–3864 2639

AFRICA

Global Museum, Maua Close Nairobi, Kenya.
Tel: 254–20–3743572

Inner Space, 28 Judith Street Johannesburg, South Africa.
Tel: 27–11–487 2800

ASIA

17 Dragon Road, Causeway Bay
Hong Kong SAR. Tel: 852–2806 3008

1-30-15 Numabukuro Tokyo, Japan.
Tel: 81–3–5380 4169

52 Lorong Melayu, Singapore.
Tel: 65–6441 1411

Chaengwattana Rd. 27, Pakkret
Bangkok, Thailand. Tel: 66–2–573 8242

7484 Bagtikan Corner, Makati City
Manila, Philippines. Tel: 63–2–890 7960

AUSTRALIA & NEW ZEALAND

78 Alt Street, Ashfield
Sydney, NSW. Tel: 61-2-9716 7066

4 Park Avenue, Avalon
Wellington. Tel: 64-4-567 0699